HOLY WAR, JUST WAR

HOLY WAR, JUST WAR

ISLAM AND CHRISTENDOM AT WAR
by *Roberto de Mattei*

Chronicles Press
Rockford, Illinois
2007

Library of Congress Cataloging-in-Publication Data

ISBN 978-0-9720616-5-0

CONTENTS

HOLY WAR, JUST WAR

Foreword

by Karl Keating

I think it was Leo XIII who remarked that "nothing is so salutary as to view the world as it really is." That was good advice in the late 19th century, and it is urgent advice in the early 21st. "To view the world as it really is" is not easy when our country's leaders try to explain the world not through ideas and principles but through slogans. We are told — in inaugural addresses, for example — that Muslim terrorists hate America because they hate America's freedoms. We are not told just which freedoms they hate. Do these terrorists think that Americans ought not to be able to "petition the government for a redress of grievances," ought not to have "freedom of speech," ought not to be secure "against unreasonable searches and seizures"?

We are not told because anyone who gives thought to the matter realizes that Muslim terrorists do not much care whether we enjoy such freedoms. Their list of complaints does not include a denunciation of the Bill of Rights. Their dissatisfaction with America in particular and the West in general does not arise from a disparagement of this freedom or that. Furthermore, they do not discriminate between legal systems arising out of British common law and those arising out of the Code Napoleon. They do not care whether we follow the principle of "one man, one vote" or the hallowed methodology of Cook County. They have no great interest in the political arrangements the countries of the West choose for themselves. These are not the things that have turned them against us.

There is a different animus at work, and it is an animus that is not peculiar to Muslim terrorists but is found, in greater or lesser degrees, in nearly all Muslims (at least in the ones who take their faith seriously). The anti-Western animus is integral to Islam itself. It is, in truth, an anti-Christian animus. Our leaders and the chattering classes may insist that Islam thinks highly of Jesus and His Mother and therefore is Christophilic, yet the more salient fact is that Islam thinks ill of Christian distinctives in general — and with good reason, given its premises.

Most Muslims understand what most Christians do not: The foundational tenets of Christianity cannot be squared with those of Islam. The one professes a triune and personal God, One Who loves His Creation and Who is so involved in its superintendence that He even humbled Himself to become man. The other professes an impersonal watchmaker God who is to be obeyed but who does not love, who demands prayer but does not answer it, who is more aloof from his creation than Dives was from Lazarus.

There is a further distinction that escapes most people in the West. Christianity is a religion, but Islam is more than a religion. It is an ideology. It is a religion conjoined with a politics, and the two cannot be separated. The religion part of Islam cannot survive without the politics part. Islam is a package deal. A Christian can go through life with nary a political thought (and, nowadays, it might be wished that more Christians would do so), but a Muslim's religious thoughts are always political, and his political thoughts are always religious. *Sharia*, for example, may be understood to be religion as applied law or law as applied religion. Even when, in the West, ecclesiastical leaders served as political leaders, there was a real and ineradicable distinction between the two swords. Under Islam, there can be but one sword.

In the following pages, Roberto de Mattei argues that "The best way to approach Islam is to respect it. And to respect it means to accept it for what it is, without 'reinterpreting' it and trying to make it what it is not." His is such a sensible approach that it unlikely to be taken up by our leaders, because to view Islam "as it really is" involves jettisoning illusions upon which our foreign policy has been built for decades. Our leaders suffer from a lack of understanding, a lack of imagination, and a lack of will. They are content to serve as justification for Robert Louis Stevenson's remark that man does not live by bread alone, but chiefly by catchwords. Their thinking is that, with catchwords, we can muddle along—and we can, for a while. The true catch is that, once that while is over, it may be too late to rectify things.

Introduction

The September 11, 2001, attack on the Twin Towers in Manhattan imprinted a dramatic seal on the new century. Osama bin Laden is clearly only the tip of an iceberg whose existence was revealed that day but whose magnitude and depth have yet to be discovered. The elimination of the Al Qaeda network will not close the conflict begun by this event, which marks the end of more than a half-century of apparent peace and prosperity following World War II.

The specter of war is looming again over the horizon, opening up scenarios that seemed to have been dismissed forever: The scenario emerging today is that of a global war which will make use of the most sophisticated technological tools and the most ruthlessly destructive weapons. Today, in the opinion of many historians, we are indeed threatened by a "clash of civilizations" along religious, political, and cultural lines, the definitive negation of the "end of ideologies" and "perpetual peace on earth" thesis.

The term "clash of civilizations" is not a palatable one in political and media circles. Those who dislike the phrase play upon an ambiguity, suggesting that those who use the term actually encourage conflict. The existence of conflict, however, is independent of both our sentiments and our diction. If only we could shun war by refusing to identify those who attack us as the enemy: It is more often the case that, by declaring war, the enemy chooses us.

When at war, it is important to identify sides, to know our enemy, to be clearly aware of the values we want to defend. To do so we must reflect on our vision of the world and our value system. This reflection, however indispensable, is not explored in this study. The following pages presuppose that we have already chosen the side of Christian civilization, in which can be found the authentic peace that is the "tranquility of order"[1] as defined by Christian tradition.

I have concentrated on the problem of defending peace, rather than on the problem of peace itself—namely, the lawfulness of war against an enemy who is attacking the West, with the aim of establishing a moral and social order that is radically opposed to our history and tradition.

The problem of the legitimacy of war and its moral value is of fundamental importance to our epoch, in which the opinion-maker, the information analyst, and the religious leader, rather than the professional soldier, become the combatants par excellence; and psychological disarmament is the primary condition for defeat. "Moral rearmament," on the contrary, supposes that the combatant can be convinced that, under certain circumstances, war is just.

The first chapter of this volume summarizes the traditional Christian doctrine on just war, showing how the timeless principles of theology and morals can help us evaluate the complex problems posed by developments in modern wars.

The second chapter describes the history and doctrine of jihad, the Islamic holy war. Today, in the name of "dialogue," Western political leaders are trying to downplay the meaning attributed to jihad by orthodox Islam. They are making a tragic mistake. The best way to approach Islam is to respect it. And to respect it means to accept it or reject it for what it is, without "reinterpreting" it and trying to make it what it is not.

The premises of modern thought, rooted in the Enlightenment, lead some to equate jihad with that form of Christian just war that is called Crusade. In the third chapter of this essay, I discuss the peculiar features of the Christian Crusade, starting with its distinctive difference from the Islamic jihad.

The Crusades are more than an historical event. The devout sacrifice of martyrs is a perennial category of the Christian spirit. I am convinced that the worst enemy of our civilization today is not attacking from the outside but from the inside, by undermining our cultural and moral defenses. Only within the framework of the Christian spirit of combat and in the traditional doctrine of the "just war"—above all, at a cultural and moral level—will the West be able to find its victory by defending its identity, and, in victory, be able to find peace.

Endnotes

[1] St. Augustine of Hippo, *De Civitate Dei* (Rome: Città Nuova, 1978-1991), book XIX, ch. 13.

The Christian Just War

Charlemagne: Model of Christian Sovereign and Warrior

December 25, 800, is a crucial date in the history of the Church and the Christian West. The coronation of Charlemagne by Pope St. Leo III on Christmas Eve of that year forged a social configuration for Christendom that became an historical model. On December 16, 2000, during a congress in the Vatican to celebrate the 1,200th anniversary of Charlemagne's coronation, John Paul II stressed the historical importance of that event, recalling the cultural and religious work done by the great emperor who was, with St. Benedict, the father of Christian Europe.[1]

The coronation of Charlemagne was a demonstration of the Gospel's political theology, which is set forth in the epistles of the Apostles Ss. Peter and Paul. This doctrine can be summarized in two points: the principle of the foundation of authority, expressed by the maxim *"Non est potestas nisi a Deo"* (Romans 13:1); and that of the distinction between spiritual and earthly domains, expressed by our Lord's commandment to "Render therefore unto Caesar the things which are Caesar's; and unto God the things that are God's" (Matthew 22:21).

The first principle, that "there is no power but of God," embodies the metaphysical foundation of any sovereignty. Each earthly sovereignty, from the family to the state, is part of the divine sovereignty, and divine and natural laws are its ultimate yardstick.

The second principle must be viewed in light of the first: Jesus Christ makes clear that, on Earth, two supreme authorities coexist — one spiritual, the other temporal. The two sovereign spheres, though distinct, are tied by a cooperative and subordinate relation expressed by the act of coronation, through which an earthly authority receives the symbols of power from the spiritual one.

The nature of this relation was described in the fifth century by Pope Gelasius (492-96) in the formula of the *duo luminaria*, according to which "there are two main powers through which the world is ruled: the sacred authority of pontiffs and the royal power."[2] For five centuries, the Christian civilization born of Charlemagne had as its ultimate references these supreme powers, wielding a *plena potestas* deriving from God directly or indirectly to either of them: the *auctoritas sacrata* of pontiffs, or *Ecclesia*, and the *regalis potestas* of sovereigns, or *Imperium*.

In the royal and imperial coronation ceremonies that followed Charlemagne's, the sovereign received from the consecrator not only the crown but the sword: *Accipe gladium de altare sumptum;* "the sword is as holy as the altar from which it is taken" and must be used only for holy causes. The sovereign was expected to brandish it vigorously to show his determination to defend the Church against any enemies, external or internal.[3]

The first of these important liturgical documents of the royal coronation ceremonies, dating as far back as the ninth century, wishes the emperor to be "*triumphator hostium ad opprimendos rebelles et paganas nationes*" — triumphant over his enemies in crushing down the rebels and pagan peoples.[4] Also dating to this epoch is the *Missa pro rege contra paganos* (Mass for the King Against Pagans), which is found in the sacrament of Angouleme and seems to be the first of a long series of Masses against pagans, compiled on the occasion of Charlemagne's campaign against the Avars.[5]

With the figure of Charlemagne, a new prototypical Christian emerges alongside the model of the martyr: that of the Christian warrior in charge of defending Christendom, the Catholic Faith, and the Church against their enemies and to ensure, also with the help of weapons, their triumph.[6]

In the Carolingian model, we find already the elements of the Christian just war and of the kind of holy war later termed Crusade. Gratian devoted the II Quaestio in the XXIII causa of his *Decretum* to definitions and formulas of war describing just war in the following terms: "*Justum est bellum, quod ex edicto geritur de rebus repetendis, aut propulsandorum hostium causa.*"[7] The first canon, inspired by Cicero and taken from Isodore of Seville by way of Ivo of Chartres, defines the just war as one waged by an edict either to recover lost goods or to repel an enemy attack. "That a just war repels an enemy attack was and has remained fundamental to all such formulating,"[8] Frederick H. Russell remarks. Just war is that which earthly kings may wage; holy war is promoted by the Pope or, in any case, leveled in defense of the Church and Christendom.

Charlemagne and Orlando are among the combatants for the faith that Dante places in the fifth Heaven of Paradise, Mars, near the spirits of Joshua, Judas Maccabeus, and the main protagonists of the Crusades.[9] For her part, the Church endorses veneration for the "just" and "warrior" king by authorizing devotion to the "blessed Charlemagne" in the diocese of Aachen.[10]

Christians and the Military in the First Centuries

The model of the Christian sovereign and warrior before Charlemagne is embodied by another emperor, Constantine the Great (d. 337). On the eve of the battle of Ponte Milvio, *ad Saxa Rubra*, on October 28, 312, he had a vision of a cross shining in the heavens with the inscription: *in hoc signo vinces*. During the night, Christ appeared to him in a dream, instructing him to adopt that very same symbol for the battle the following day.

Constantine's victory ended the age of persecutions, opening a new era in the history of the Church. It is in the military and thanks to it that, as rightly pointed out by Henri Leclercq, Christianity gains its first public recognition.[11]

Despite Tertullian's opinions to the contrary, opinions that clearly reflect his evolution toward the Montanist heresy,[12] no act of the Magisterium had ever prohibited a Christian from undertaking military service in the first three centuries. On the contrary, many Christians served as officers or soldiers in the Roman legions without reproach from the Church, reconciling the two aspects of being Christians and soldiers; some of them were even canonized.[13] This is all the more significant since the military draft in the Roman Empire was neither universal nor compulsory, except in exceptional situations.[14]

The case of St. Maximilian, who, in 295, preferred to die rather than to serve in the army, is an isolated one. Christian officers and soldiers who were martyred during this period were not put to death for having refused as Christians to bear weapons but for having refused to commit idolatry and apostasy by participating in pagan ceremonies.[15] Such were the examples of St. Eustachio, St. Sebastian, St. Maurice, and the Legio XII *Fulminata* under Marcus Aurelius, as well as of the Theban Legion under Diocletian and Maximian.

Constantine's victory and the Edict of Milan, issued in February 313, ended the age of persecutions. The Christian doctrine of the just war originated from the subsequent christianization of Roman society and institutions and the birth of the Christian state. The third Canon of the Council of Arles, held in August 313, a few months following the Edict of Milan, condemns pacifism for the first time, stating that "those who throw away their weapons be excommunicated."[16]

"Defeat, O God, the enemies of the Roman name and Catholic creed!" reads the *Sacramentario Leoniano*, which was compiled in Rome in the fifth or sixth century. "Protect everywhere the rulers of Rome, for Your people to have safe peace with their victory! Destroy the enemies of Your people! Defend the stability of the Roman name and protect its domination, so that lasting peace and good reign among your peoples!"[17]

The idea of the legitimacy of certain wars and the celebration of the Christian soldier made even more sense during the long centuries of barbarian invasions, laden with violence and horrors that the Church sought to alleviate with her teaching and example. The Church did not teach pacifism to these invaders, but the ideal of the Christian warrior.

St. Augustine's Theory of Just War

The first elaboration of the Christian doctrine on war is to be found in St. Augustine (354-430), mainly in book XIX of the *City of God*.[18] His theories inspired all medieval elaborations on the subject and are still to be kept in serious consideration.

In the first place, St. Augustine teaches that all men crave peace; those who wage war desire only to assure peace through victory; "peace, therefore, is the ultimate purpose of waging war. Every man wants peace, even when waging a war; on the contrary, no one wants war while he is at peace."[19] Not every peace is just, however. There is false and apparent peace, and then there is the true peace which is the "tranquility of order"[20] — namely, the correct disposition of all things under the principles of natural and divine law.

The bishop of Hippo's thought unfolds as follows:

1. War is an evil to which, nonetheless, it is sometimes necessary to resort in order to restore just peace and avoid more serious evils.

2. War may be "just" if the peace toward which it tends is just. In a famous passage, St. Augustine defines the *iusta bella*, the "just wars," with the following words: "wars that revenge injustices are defined as just: and that is when a people or a city ought to be wiped out for having omitted to chastise the ill deeds of their subjects, or to give back what had been taken away unjustly."[21] It is important to note in this passage that what makes a war just is the iniquity of the opposing side. The war is just because an injustice has been or is being done.

3. Our will must always tend toward the good of peace. War is fought out of necessity, so that God may free us from an injustice and pre-serve us in peace. War is waged in order to achieve peace. "Therefore be peaceful in waging war, so to prompt those whom you must fight against, into the good of peace with your victory. Says in fact our Lord: 'the peaceful be blessed, for they will be called children of God (Matthew 5:9).'"[22]

As to the suffering that results from war and sometimes afflicts the innocent, it is permitted by God for His providential purposes of mercy, salvation, and sanctification; God Who "directs the beginning, the unfolding and end of wars."[23] "A just war, moreover, is justified only by the injustice of an aggressor; and that injustice ought to be a source of grief to any good man, because it is human injustice. It would be deplorable in itself, apart from being a source of conflict. Any man who will consider sorrowfully evils so great, such horrors and such savagery, will admit his human misery. And if there is any man who can endure such calamities, or even contemplate them without feeling grief, his condition is all the more wretched for that. For it is only the loss of all humane feeling that could make him call such a life 'the happy life.'"[24]

St. Thomas Aquinas's Theory of Just War

The judgment of St. Thomas Aquinas (1225-74) on war is of the utmost importance, not only for its intrinsic value but for the influence it has subsequently exerted on the doctrine of the Church.[25] The ideas of the Angelic Doctor are set forth above all in the *Secunda Secundae* section of the *Summa Theologica*, where he explores the Christian virtues.

St. Thomas explicitly talks of *iustum bellum*, drawing on St. Augustine's main conception, according to which "those who wage just war aim at peace. Therefore they only oppose evil peace, which the Lord has not come to bring on to earth (Matthew 10:34)." Also, the one who seeks war, St. Thomas writes, desires peace, which he believes he does not have, but since there can be no real peace other than in the desire for real good, "true peace is only to be found in good men and in good things, on the contrary, the peace of the wicked is not a true peace but a semblance thereof."[26]

The three classic conditions for just war, as set out by St. Thomas, are as follows:First, war must be declared by a competent authority: "For it is not the business of a private individual to declare war, because he can seek for redress of his rights from the tribunal of his superior."[27]. St. Thomas recalls a quotation by St. Augustine: "the natural order, suitable for peace among mortals, demands that the authority and the deliberation to resort to war be vested in the Princes."[28]

Second, a just cause is required — namely, "a guilt on the part of those against whom war is waged." St. Thomas again echoes St. Augustine here: "wars that revenge injustices are defined as just: and that is when a people or a city ought to be wiped out for having omitted to chastise the ill deeds of their subjects, or to give back what had been taken away unjustly."[29]

Third, the just intention of those who fight is required — namely, "that the aim be to promote good and shun evil." Once again, St. Thomas recalls St. Augustine's words: "among the real worshippers of God also wars are peaceful, which are not waged for greed or cruelty, but for the love of peace, that is to repress the wicked and aid the good." Therefore "the lust to harm, the cruelty in the revenge, the implacable indignation, the ferocity in combating, the frenzy to overpower and other things of this kind are justly condemned in war."[30]

"This doctrine by St. Thomas," writes Father de la Brière, "is confirmed, indirectly but clearly, by pontifical bulls and Medieval conciliar decrees regarding the peace of God, the truce of God, and the peaceful settlement, or by means of mediation, of conflicts between kingdoms. These documents expound the authentic doctrine of the Church and the general spirit of her teaching on moral questions regarding peace and war rights."[31]

It should be noted that the just war of which St. Thomas and St. Augustine write is an offensive war. Defensive war is one of the natural rights of men to self-defense and, in the opinion of these authors, does not need to be justified judicially or theologically: "*Vim vi repellere omnia iura permittunt.*"[32]

Offensive wars, when they are just (e.g., those waged to recover a lost province or city, to punish another nation for assisting the enemy, to help allies, or to punish treaty violators), cannot be called aggressive. Resorting to arms in an offensive war is based on the justice of vengeance,[33] whose nature is described by St.

Thomas in a *quaestio* of the *Summa Theologica*.[34]

The instinct for revenge, he explains, being an action of natural repulsion in the face of evil, must contain something good; the *vindicatio*, the "just revenge," is therefore licit, provided that the primary goals be the correction of the culprit (rather than the harming of him) or "the repression of evil for the good of public order, the safeguarding the right and doing honour to God."[35] Therefore, the holy and virtuous man "repels what is harmful by defending himself, either warding off injuries, or, if they have already been inflicted, avenging them, not with the intention of doing harm but of repelling an injustice."[36]

Just War and the Second Scholastics

The doctrine of the offensive just war, after St. Augustine and St. Thomas, was developed under many aspects by the great Spanish scholars of the Second Scholastics, the Dominican Francisco de Vitoria (1492-1546) and, above all, the Jesuit Francisco de Suárez (1508-1617), also known as the Doctor Eximius, who devotes the XIII *disputatio* of his treatise *De Charitate* to this very subject. He maintains that war "is not in itself intrinsically evil, nor prohibited to Christians, this is a truth of faith contained in the Holy Scriptures, since in the Old Testament wars waged by very holy men are praised: 'Blessed be Abraham by God Almighty, creator of heaven and earth, and blessed be God Almighty for His protection handed over your enemies to you' (Genesis 14:20).[37] Similar passages can be found regarding Moses, Joshua, Samson, Gideon, David, the Maccabeus and others, men whom God ordered many times to wage wars against enemies of the Jews; and St. Paul says that these saints have conquered empires in honour of the faith. The same is confirmed by other testimonies of the Holy Fathers quoted by Gratian, as well as by St. Ambrose in several chapters of his book on duties."[38]

The defensive war, and here the Jesuit scholar echoes Vitoria, repels an unjust aggression, while this is being inflicted. Aggressive and offensive wars, however, are waged to repair an injustice that has already occurred. The distinction is made by determining who resorted to force in the first place. In a defensive war, those committing the injustice have taken the initiative, and those who wage war are compelled to defend themselves; in an offensive war, the initiative is taken by those who have already suffered injustice and who, after having used all other means to seek reparation, resort to force.[39] Aggressive war is not invariably evil "but can be honest and necessary,"[40] provided no other means is effective and that the injury suffered is of such a serious nature so to justify resorting to such a consequence-laden means of redressing it."[41]

Just War: Pros and Cons

One objection to a Christian just war would seem to come from the universal natural and divine precept expounded in the Fifth Commandment: "Thou shalt not kill." The Church's traditional response is that the commandment does not refer to killing in itself but to the murder of the innocent. Guilt demands a reparatory justice, exercised by the public authority, just as aggression legitimizes defense, which Church doctrine allows even a private person to exercise.

To the question, "Are there cases in which to kill is legitimate?" the Catechism of St. Pius X replied: "It is licit to kill one's fellowman when a just war is fought, when the death penalty as a sentence for some offenses is carried out by order of the supreme authority, and, finally, when defense is necessary against an unjust aggressor."[42] The new Catechism of the Catholic Church substantially confirms this doctrine.[43]

Pacifists may cite other objections drawn from passages in the Gospel, such as this one: "Put up again thy sword into his place: for all they that take the sword shall perish with the sword" (Matthew 26:52). Jesus is rebuking Peter, however, because he drew his sword on impulse alone and without being authorized by the Lord. "All that arm themselves against the blood of somebody else," St. Augustine explains, "take the sword without the command or permission of any legitimate and superior power"[44]; he who uses the sword by order of God or of the competent authority, St. Thomas remarks, does not bear the sword by his own right.[45] Therefore, what Jesus prohibits here is the undue use of the sword, which in that moment was unjustified. He does not forbid all use of a sword, and, in fact, He Himself authorized the Apostles to bear one.

Far from condemning war, natural law and the Gospel offer the doctrinal arguments for it to be regarded as legitimate under the right circumstances.

War, explains Francisco de Vitoria,[46] was permitted by natural law, as can be seen in the Old Testament: In fact, nowhere in it is war condemned; on the contrary, the Old Testament relates of both the just war of defense and liberation and the just war of aggression and conquest. The just war is explicitly attributed to God's will: The people of Israel fight in His name, under His mandate, relying on His help, against His enemies. Abraham wages war against four kings (Genesis 14); in the book of Numbers, there is a reference to the "Book of the wars of the Lord," an ancient collection of national and religious songs (Numbers 21:14); Deuteronomy tells us not to be saddened by the plight of vanquished enemies (Deuteronomy 7:16); Judges celebrates the victories of Israel (Judges 3:29-31, 4:16, 8:10). After having dictated the Fifth Commandment to Moses, God lists a long series of sins that are to be punished by death: For example, "whoever hits somebody causing his death will have to be put to death" (Exodus 21:12).

In the New Testament, when Jesus was hit by a servant in front of the high priest, He did not "turn the other cheek" but defended Himself by arguing, "If there is something wrong in what I said, point it out; but if there is no offense in it, why do you strike me?" (John 18:23). When some soldiers asked John the Baptist how they should behave, he replied: "Do not make violence on anybody, neither slander and be content with your pay" (Luke 3:14). Therefore, St. Augustine argues, if John the Baptist ordered them to be content with their pay, he was not forbidding them to be soldiers.[47]

Nor are soldiers depicted in the New Testament as in some way lesser members of the faithful. Impressed by the faith of the Roman centurion in Capernaum, whose servant He healed, Jesus exclaimed: "I say unto you, I have not found so great faith, no, not in Israel" (Luke 7:6-9), and it is a centurion's voice on Golgotha that acknowledges the divinity of Jesus — "*Vere filius Dei erat iste*" (Matthew 27:54); and Cornelius, a centurion of the Italian Cohort stationed in Caesarea, had the privilege of being visited by an angel and baptized by St. Peter (Acts 10:1-48).

The misunderstanding at the background of a pacifist reading of the New Testament is attributable to the transposition to the social and political level of certain precepts of Jesus Christ that are of a purely moral nature. "By the same token, in the name of the Sermon of the mountain, private property, tribunals and all organs of a hierarchical society, as well as war and military service, would have to be excluded."[48]

When Christ told us to offer the other cheek, He proposed a high ideal of personal perfection that also includes, and at times imposes, the right and the duty of individuals to defend themselves from aggressors, especially when the common good is at stake. In another passage, Christ said that, "if the goodman of the house had known in what watch the thief would come, he would have watched, and would not have suffered his house to be broken up" (Matthew 24:43). These words compel the family father, as well as the head of state whose position is analogous to the head of the family, to defend his charges against unjust aggressors — even, if necessary, by resorting to organized armed force.[49]

The traditional doctrine on war, as taught by the Church over the last millennium, can be summarized as follows: War in itself, as the use of force, is neither intrinsically good nor intrinsically evil. It becomes good or evil, just or unjust, according to the aims it intends to achieve. War made without a just cause and in an unjust manner is illicit; on the other hand, war is legitimate — and, indeed, in some cases, is required — when is waged with a just cause and in a just manner. In particular:

1. A defensive war against an unjust aggressor is always legitimate, for nations have, like individuals, a natural right to their own defense.

2. For an offensive war to be just, it:
    a. must have as its primary goal the restoration of a right seriously infringed upon or the reparation of a grave wrong suffered;
    b. must be the last means to which the state resorts to safeguard a right;
    c. must entail a just proportion between the evils that it produces and the importance of the right it is meant to defend.

Therefore, in St. Augustine's and St. Thomas's doctrine of just war, the *auctoritas principis* and the *recta intentio* — namely, that a war be declared by the legitimate authority ruling the state and that said authority act with the right intention — must to be added to the *iusta causa* that justifies intervention.

The Characteristics of Modern War

For over a millennium, the Church constantly taught that war waged for a just cause was legitimate. The characteristics of war in the 20th century, however, have posed serious moral questions that deserve to be carefully explored.

The century of totalitarianism saw the advent of mass wars, with characteristics quite different from traditional ones. After the end of World War II, Pope Pius XII said, "modern progress has conceived and manufactured such inhuman and deadly weapons that can destroy not only fleets and armies, not only cities, towns and villages and priceless treasures of religion, art and culture, but also the innocent children with their mothers, the sick and the old. All that is good, beautiful and holy which has been produced by the human genius, it can all, or almost all, be destroyed."[50]

In particular, modern war involves the whole population without making any distinction, in principle, between combatants and civilians; threatens the total annihilation of the enemy, thanks to the technical characteristics of modern weapons; and is total in the sense that it is no longer confined to a limited territory but tends to become global.

In the light of these problems, the Church has developed and restated Her doctrine as follows. First, the moral imperative of the Church is peace, which is "a divine command."[51] However, peace "is not merely the absence of war, and is not limited to maintaining a balance of powers between adversaries."[52] It is the Augustinian "tranquility of order," "the work of justice," and "the effect of charity."[53] "Peace," says Pope Pius XII, "is very different from a mere humanitarian sentiment, which all too often is nothing but an extreme sensitivity which detests war only because of its horrors and atrocities, its havoc and its dire consequences, but not also because of its injustice. Such a sentiment, hedonistic and utilitarian in character, and materialistic in origin, lacks the firm foundation of a strict and unconditional obligation and it forms the kind of soil in which the deceit of sterile compromise and the attempt to save oneself at the cost of others take root, and in every case, it guarantees the success of the aggressor."[54]

Second, the traditional doctrine of the just war, both defensive and offensive, has not changed in principle. In practice, however, the nature of modern war seems to make modern offensive war illicit. The devastation that can result from an offensive war waged with modern weapons seems disproportionate to any good results such a war may achieve.

On the other hand, both the law and Catholic doctrine[55] confirm the legitimacy of defensive war under certain conditions, as confirmed by Pope Pius XII:

If any people threatened with, or already the victim of, an unjust aggression, wants to think and act in a Christian way, it cannot remain passively indifferent. All the more does the solidarity of the family of peoples forbid the other members to behave like simple onlookers with an attitude of unconcerned neutrality. . . . So true is this that neither the mere consideration of the sorrows and evils resulting from war, nor the exact balancing of action and advantage, suffice for a final decision whether it is morally lawful or, in a given concrete case, morally binding, to resist the aggressor resorting to the use of force (provided there is a well-founded likelihood of success). . . .

Their defense is furthermore an obligation for the nations as a whole who have a duty not to abandon a nation that is attacked. The certainty that this duty will not go unfulfilled will serve to discourage the aggressor and thus war will be avoided or, if the worst should come, its sufferings will at least be lessened."[56]

This is the very same right to individual self-defense applied to peoples and states. An individual may choose not to exercise this right for himself; the state, however, has a duty to protect the common good of its citizens, which consists not only of material assets but of the legacy of values and principles that constitutes society, such as the fundamental rights and liberties of man and, above all else, the Christian Faith and morals. The importance of certain spiritual and moral goods — such as faith, justice, and liberty — fully warrants their defense by force against unjust aggression.

Pius XII's doctrine on just war has been confirmed by the Second Vatican Council, the speeches of Pope John Paul II, and by the Catechism of the Catholic Church, according to which, "as long as the danger of war persists and there is no international authority with the necessary competence and power, governments cannot be denied the right to lawful self-defense, once all peace efforts have failed."[57] The Catechism, in its 1997[58] *editio typica*, at paragraph 2265, replaces the term just war with that of *legitimate defense*, defining it as follows:

Legitimate defense, besides being a right, may even be a serious duty for those who are responsible for other people's lives. The defense of common good calls for the unjust aggressor to be put in a position of not harming anybody. In this regard the legitimate authorities are entitled to resort also to arms if necessary in order to fend off the aggressors of the community of civilians for which they are responsible.

The Conditions for a Just War in the Modern Age

To sum up, a just war is moral when it is waged by a legitimate authority, defending itself against an unjust and present aggression — in other words, when it serves a justice that another party has rejected, offended, or destroyed.

Defense is legitimate both when an injustice has already occurred and when it is about to be carried out[59] — that is, not only when an attack by an enemy is under way but when the attack is inevitable[60] and already begun, even with the use of nonconventional weapons or acts of terrorism. The conditions for a just war in the present time, according to the new Catechism,[61] are the following:

1. that all other means to end the aggression have failed or proved impracticable;

2. that the aggressor must not be harmed more than is necessary;

3. that those waging the defensive war must have a good chance to succeed and must not risk assets more valuable than those being protected.

Moreover, the Church and human reason alike maintain that the moral law still stands during armed conflicts: "the mere fact that war has regrettably broken out does not mean that everything becomes licit between the warring parties."[62] Furthermore, "actions deliberately contrary to the law of nations and to its universal principles are crimes, as are the orders that command such actions. Blind obedience does not suffice to excuse those who carry them out."[63]In its inception, development, and end, war is to be regulated not just by military requirements but by what is right,for the law of justice is more important than the opposite interests of the warring parties. Justice cannot be separated from charity, which commands us to love and benefit our fellowmen, enemies included, according to the words of Christ: "But I say unto you which hear, Love your enemies, do good to them which hate you.". This means that, even if it is licit, in the case of just war, to damage an enemy for a just cause, it is immoral to hate him.

Furthermore, those who wage war must maintain the highest possible degree of concern for civilians, who, under no circumstances, should ever be attacked intentionally. When attacking military targets, it is possible that civilians may be involved, but it is necessary that all precautions be taken to lessen the dire effects of such occurrence.

Nuclear, Bacteriological, and Chemical Weapons and "Postmodern" Wars

The modern age has seen the birth and development of atomic, biological, and chemical (ABC) weapons, which are different from conventional ones not only because of their power but by their very nature. In fact, they are:

1. the means of undifferentiated destruction that harms innocents, or even combatants, disproportionately to any possible good resulting from war, which becomes nothing but a real act of destruction and extermination.

2. much less under the power and control of men than traditional weapons, with regard both to their destination and to their consequences. Those who use such weapons are unable to foresee the ultimate consequences of their actions.

The more often modern weapons are used, the more war becomes a brutal destruction and completely inhuman. We must consider, therefore, the possibility that the use of such weapons could always be regarded as immoral, be it in defensive or in aggressive war.

In a number of his speeches, Pope Pius XII posed this very same question — whether the ABC war is ever to be considered simply necessary when resorting to it in defense against an aggressor who makes use of such weapons — and urged us to argue the answer "from the same principles which are decisive in determining the justification of war in general."[64]

Is the modern "total war," and the ABC war in particular, ever to be permitted by principle? — this is the Pontiff's question.

There can be no doubt, mainly because of the horrors and unlimited sufferings caused by modern warfare, that to unleash such warfare without a just cause — that is to say, without its being justified by an obvious and extremely grave injustice that cannot otherwise be repelled — would be a "crime" deserving of the most severe national and international sanctions. In principle it is wrong even to ask if atomic, bacteriological and chemical warfare is lawful except when such warfare must be deemed indispensable for defense in the conditions previously indicated. And even then, however, all means must be used to try to avoid it through international agreements, or, at least, to place upon its use such well-defined and rigid limitations as will guarantee that its effects will be confined to the strict needs of defense. Moreover, should the evil consequences of setting this method of warfare in motion ever become so widespread as to elude human control completely, then its use must be rejected as immoral. It would then no longer be a question of "defense" against injustice and of the necessary "safeguarding" of lawful possessions, but of the pure and simple annihilation of all human life within the radius of the destructive action. This is not permissible on any account.[65]

Therefore, an ABC war is permitted only in response to an evident and extremely serious injustice that cannot be redressed otherwise and only if it is possible to keep its effects, to some degree, under control. The most self-assured moralists maintain that only one motive can warrant the use of modern weapons — namely, that the aggressor uses them and that there is no other means by which a threatened state may save itself.[66] In other words, modern ABC weapons may be used only for a just defensive war and only in extreme circumstances for legitimate self–defense.[67]

The greatest modern transformation of the nature of war, however, does not concern the quantity and quality of weapons but the disappearance of the traditional political entities—namely, the states—that Catholic doctrine recognizes as the only legitimate authorities with the power to declare and conduct war.

Following the fall of the Berlin Wall in 1989, a process of disintegration of the nation-state started, led, on the one hand, by international organisms such as the United Nations, the European Union, NATO, and others, and, on the other, by interstate bodies such as non-governmental organizations (NGOs) and transnational associations of various kinds. These include criminal and terrorist lobbies as well as religious groups, such as the Islamic Jihad. As traditional states have lost or surrendered their power to these international organizations and groups, modern wars—be they "asymmetrical" wars waged by these groups and lobbies or "humanitarian" wars waged by international organizations—are not only without "just cause" or "right intention" but without a legitimate state or authority to declare them. Like no other type of war, the modern one defies the rule of the three requirements necessary for a war to be defined as "just"—namely, *auctoritas principis*, *iusta causa*, and *recta intentio*.

"Humanitarian" Wars

"Humanitarian" wars are those waged by international entities in order to redress "crimes against humanity" and violations of "human rights" within the national and geographic boundaries of a self-governing state, such as Kosovo in 1999. They have given birth to the International Criminal Court and to an "international police force" that prosecutes all violators of human rights, or so-called human rights, in the name of a "right of ethical interference."

Catholic doctrine does not acknowledge the justice of offensive war—even in the name of "humanitarian interference"—waged without a state mandate and outside the norms of natural and Christian law, whereas it maintains that a state has a right to self-defense, when it is under attack. In the case of the Kosovo war, NATO intervened without so much as the endorsement of the United Nations and imposed a political solution on the territory of a state whose sovereignty had not been officially challenged. The declared aim of this military campaign was to avoid a "humanitarian catastrophe," but that is precisely what was made worse after the beginning of the bombardments. NATO's military victory there has become an ethical and political defeat, as the Balkans have become increasingly unstable.[68] Judging the Kosovo war by either its premises or its consequences, it is hard to describe this type of "humanitarian war" as morally just.

A legitimate supranational authority, to which all states could be subject, does not yet exist. Recent Pontiffs had hoped that the United Nations would one day be able to perform such a role.[69] However, the fact that this has not happened is now generally acknowledged. Even if such an authority were in place and had the power to force all states to abide by what it should declare just, it would still have to define the legal and moral principles that would constitute the benchmark for its standards of justice. "Human rights," which are so often referred to nowadays, are not in fact traditional human rights, which originate from an objective natural order, but new rights or pseudo-rights, founded on an unrestricted exertion of freedom.

Pope Pius IX condemns the absolute principle of nonintervention, and Pope Pius XII teaches that, sometimes, "to intervene is a duty and neutrality a mistake."[70] This right certainly extends to an international community consisting of a family of sovereign nations that recognize a common moral authority (such as the papacy in Christian Europe), and a common natural law inscribed on the human heart (Romans 2:14). What right of intervention, however, could be claimed by a supranational authority that does not recognize any supreme moral authority or objective norms of natural law and that appeals to the "ethics" of "humanitarian interference" in the name of a relativist ideology, so as to speed up the pace of the dissolution of nations and states and to impose such anti-rights as abortion and homosexuality?[71]

Where can the *iusta causa* and the *auctoritas principis* be found here?

"Asymmetrical" Wars

Alongside the "humanitarian" war, there is a new type of war: the so-called asymmetrical wars that are chaotic or "nonlinear," when compared with the traditional political and military parameters.[72] The main feature of asymmetrical wars is that they are waged by transnational, nongoverning groups, for often ill-defined aims, and extend globally in time, space, and objectives. These groups often purposefully attack civilians because the war is directed against an enemy culture, in the name of an organization with a radically different political-religious worldview.

Psychological warfare is a fundamental component of asymmetrical war. Clausewitz, in his 1813 treatise *On War*, considered it even then to be an essential part of military conflict, and, in the 20th century, totalitarian regimes developed and expanded its use. Today, however, thanks in part to new information technology such as the Internet, the relationship between psychological warfare and traditional war has been reversed: Traditional warfare has become subsidiary to psychological war.[73] Terrorism must be evaluated on the strength of its psychological impact on society rather than by the actual destructive effects and material damages that it causes; and it must never be considered by itself but as an expression of the world vision from which it derives, even if this is more often than not of a merely destructive and nihilist nature.

From an ethical point of view, the problem of asymmetrical war is not just the indiscriminate use of the means of warfare but the very nature of the authority that resorts to them. Once again, the concept of sovereignty is at stake here — namely, the definition of who is the competent authority that can declare war or respond to it. It is not always clear nowadays who declares war and against whom. Asymmetrical wars tend to multiply in an acephalous society, and their protagonists may be hackers, stock-exchange speculators, opinion leaders, ideologists, and religious leaders. These wars often lack definite goals or frontiers, or even states, and, just like humanitarian wars, they should be considered against the background of the postmodern crisis of the concept of sovereignty.

Real Causes of, and Remedies for, Wars

All too often in our postmodern world, the devastating material and moral consequences of wars are confused with their causes. Without understanding and removing these causes, we cannot dispel the specter of destruction looming over our future.

The Magisterium of the Church teaches that the profound and real causes of war are not political and economic but spiritual and moral, and they stem from the violation of the Christian and natural order that arises from the abandonment of God's Law in national and international life.

"Let's fathom the conscience of modern Society to its bottom, let's seek the origin of evil: where is it rooted?" asks Pope Pius XII. The answer is in the "gradual individual and social de-Christianization" and "religious anaemia" which is widespread in Europe.[74]

In his encyclical *Summi pontificatus*, Pius XII states that

> the radical and ultimate cause of the evils which We deplore in modern
> society is the denial and rejection of a universal norm of morality for
> individual and social life as well as for international relations; We mean
> the disregard, which is so common nowadays, and the forgetfulness of
> the natural law itself, which has its foundation in God Almighty, Creator
> and Father of all, supreme and absolute Legislator, all-knowing and just
> Judge of human actions.[75]

Peace, Pope John Paul II confirms, originates from the "rational and moral order of all society," founded on God as "primary source of being, essential truth and supreme goodness."[76] In particular, says the pontiff, "the defense of the universality and inviolability of human rights is essential for the construction of a peaceful society and for the complete development of individuals, people and nations."[77]

For Christians, the real cause of war, as of any other evil, is sin, which breeds injustice and iniquity. While an individual faced with injustice may choose to endure evil, the state has the duty to protect the common good, which is moral and spiritual much more than it is material, and, like every good, it has to be considered as part of the ultimate and supreme Goodness, in Whose perfection it participates.

When facing a military confrontation, our essential duty is to establish whether spiritual and moral goods worthy of being defended even at the cost of the horrors of modern war are at stake in these particular circumstances.

Given a choice between legitimate goods of different natures, such as the material well-being of a nation and its moral legacy, a government leader should always prefer the superior good to the inferior one, even at the cost of sacrificing the latter in a war, always recalling the words of Judas Maccabeus: "it is better for us to die in battle than to watch the ruin of our nation and our holy sanctuary" (1 Maccabees 3:59). For Christian souls, war and death are not the worst evils. War is the worst evil only for those who adopt the irreligious vision that considers life, rather than the supreme aspiration which transcends life itself, as the supreme good.[78] On the contrary, for those who believe in the preeminence of the spiritual over the material, the balance between the evils caused by war and the good that such war is waged to defend will always be in favor of the latter, provided the right to be reestablished is worthy of it.[79]

The purpose of peace, Pope Pius XII explains, is the protection of the goods of humanity, given that they were created by God, to Whom they ultimately belong. "Now, among these [goods] are some so important for human society that their defense against unjust aggression is beyond question fully lawful."[80]

The defense of superior goods may never be achieved by means or acts that are immoral in themselves. The rules of a just war from a Christian point of view remain those of traditional morals, which do not accept the Machiavellian maxim that the end justifies the means.[81] No evil, however well intentioned, is ever excusable: "That would be the same as saying: Do evil as a means to good. Some slanderers have accused us of teaching this, but they are justly condemned" (Romans 3:8). Christians may tolerate evil, but they do not desire it; nor do they commit it, not even for grave reasons, or in order to achieve good. The aim remains the benefit of peace, and the means to be chosen to achieve this aim, even if they involve resorting to arms, will always have to be good and just. Only in this case can a war be called just and aim at restoring peace through justice: *opus iustitiae pax* (Isaiah 32:17).

Endnotes

[1] John Paul II, "Message dated 14 December 2000," *Osservatore Romano*, 51 (2000), p. 5.

[2] Gelasius, *Epistula VIII ad Anastasium Imperatorem* (PL, 59, col. 42).

[3] Michael Villey, *La Croisade. Essai sur la formation d'une theorie juridique* (Paris: Vrin, 1942), p. 39; Anna Maria Morisi, *La guerra nel pensiero cristiano dalle origini alle crociate* (Florence, Sansoni,1963), p. 179.

[4] *Ibid.*, pp. 178-9.

[5] Villey, *op. cit.*, p. 28; Morisi, *op. cit.*, p. 177.

[6] Etienne Delaruelle, "*Essai sur la formation de l'idée de croisade,*" *Bullettin de littérature ecclési-astique* 42 (1941), p. 24-25; Villey, *op. cit.*, pp. 41-46; Jean Flori, *La guerre sainte. La formation de l'idée de la Croisade dans l'Occident chrétien* (Paris: Aubier, 2001), pp. 29-34.

[7] Gratian, *Decretum, emendatum et variis lectionibus simul et notationibus illustratum,* PL, 187 (1861), causa XXIII, quaestio II, cols. 1166–67.

[8] Frederick H. Russell, *The Just War in the Middle Ages* (New York: Cambridge University Press, 1975), p. 62.

[9] Dante Alighieri, *Divina Commedia* (Milan: Rizzoli, 1995), book III, Canto 8, 43-45.

[10] Robert Folz, *Etude sur le culte liturgique de Charlemagne dans les églises de l'Empire* (Geneva: Slatkine rpt, 1973).

[11] Henri Leclercq, "*Militarisme,*" *DACL* (1933), book XI, col. 1147.

[12] *Ibid.*, cols. 1122-26.

[13] Rino Cammilleri, *I santi militari* (Casale Monferrato: Piemme, 1992), pp. 69-90.

[14] Yves de la Briere, *Le droit de juste guerre, Tradition théologique, adaptations contemporaines* (Paris: A. Pedone, 1938), pp. 14-15; Franco Cardini, *Alle radici della cavalleria medioevale* (Florence: La Nuova Italia, 1982), pp. 194-99.

[15] Briere, *Le droit de juste guerre,* p. 15.

[16] Charles Joseph Hefele, *Histoire des Conciles d'aprés les documents originaux* (Paris: Letouzey et Anè, 1907), pp. 282-83.

[17] Quoted in Carl Erdmann, *Alle origini dell'idea di crociata* (Spoleto: Centro italiano di studi sull'Alto Medioevo, 1996), pp. 31-32.

[18] Briere, *Le droit de juste guerre,* p.21-27; Flori, *op. cit.*, pp. 37-39.

[19] St. Augustine of Hippo, *De Civitate Dei* (Rome: Città Nuova, 1978-1991), book XIX, ch. 12.

[20] *Ibid.*, book XIX, ch. 13.

[21] St. Augustine of Hippo, *Quaestiones in Heptateuchum* (PL, 33) in Iosue, book IV, q. 10, col. 781.

[22] St. Augustine of Hippo, *Epistola al conte Bonifacio* (PL, 33), cols. 855-56.

[23] St. Augustine of Hippo, *De Civitate Dei*, book XIX, ch. 7.

[24] *Ibid.*, book XIX, ch. 12.

[25] Briere, *Le droit de juste guerre*, pp. 30-31.

[26] St. Thomas Aquinas, *Summa Theologica* (Bologna:Edizioni Studio Domenicano, 1984), II–IIae, quaestio 29, article 2, ad 2 and ad 3.

[27] *Ibid.*, quaestio 40, article 1, resp.

[28] St. Augustine of Hippo, *Contra Faustum Manichaeum* (PL, 42, cols. 207-518), book XXII, ch. 75, col. 448.

[29] St. Augustine of Hippo, *Quaestiones,* in Iosue, book IV, q. 10, col.781.

[30] St. Augustine of Hippo, *Contra Faustum*, book XXII, ch. 74, col 447.

[31] Yves de la Briere, *Paix et Guerre*, DAFC (1926), vol. III, col. 1262.

[32] Ulpian, *Digestum*, book 1, § 27, De vi, 43, 16.

[33] Briere, *Paix et Guerre*, vol. III, col. 1265.

[34] St. Thomas Aquinas, *Summa Theologica*, II–IIae, quaestio 108, articles 1 and 2.

[35] *Ibid.*, art 1.

[36] *Ibid.*, art 2.

[37] On the doctrine of war in the Second Scholastics, see Alfred Vanderpol, *La doctrine scolastique du droit de guerre* (Paris: A. Pedone, 1919); Carlo Giacon, S.J., *La seconda scolastica. I problemi giuridico – politici. Suarez, Bellarmino, Mariana* (Milan: Fratelli Bocca, 1950), vol. III; Luciano Perena Vicente, *Teoria de la Guerra en Francisco Suarez* (Madrid: C.S.I.C., 1954).

[38] Francisco Suarez, *Opera Omnia* (Paris: Vivés, 1856-78); Disp. XIII, *De Bello*, Section I, No.2, p. 737.

[39] *Ibid.*, No. 6, p.738.

[40] *Ibid.*, No. 4, p.738.

[41] *Ibid.*, No. 1, p.743.

[42] *Catechismo Maggiore promulgato da S. Pio X* (Milan: Ares, 1979), P. III, ch. 3, par. 2, answer to question No. 413.

[43] *Catechismo della Chiesa Cattolica* (Vatican City: Libreria Editrice Vaticana, 1992), n. 2265.

[44] St. Augustine of Hippo, *Contra Faustum*, book XXII, ch. 70, col 444.

[45] St. Thomas Aquinas, *Summa Theologica*, II–IIae, quaestio 40, article 1, ad 1.

[46] Francisco da Vitoria, *De Iure Belli* (Rome-Bari: Laterza, 2005 – Italian translation), book I.

[47] St. Augustine of Hippo, *Epistola ad Marcellinum* (PL, 33, cols. 525-535), 138, c.II, 15, col. 531.

[48] Briere, *Paix et Guerre*, col. 1258.

[49] Eberhard Welty, *Catechismo Sociale* (Francavilla, Chieti: Paoline, 1966; two volumes, Italian translation), II, p. 381.

[50] Pope Pius XII, *Discorsi e Radiomessaggi* (Vatican City: Tipografia Vaticana, 1959; 21 volumes); *Summi Maeroris* (July 19, 1950), Vol. XIII, p. 519.

[51] *Ibid.*, 1948, p. 322.

[52] *Catechismo della Chiesa Cattolica*, n. 2304.

[53] Vatican Ecumenical Council II, *Pastoral Constitution on the Church in the Modern World "Gaudium at Spes,"* (Vatican, December 7, 1965), n.78. See also *Catechismo della Chiesa Cattolica*, n. 2304.

[54] Pope Pius XII, *Discorsi e Radiomessaggi*, December 24, 1948, Vol. X, p. 322.

[55] Alfredo Ottaviani, *Institutiones iuris publici ecclesastici* (Vatican City: Typis Polyglottis Vaticanis, 1958–ed. IV, *emendata et aucta*), p. 137; Eberhard Welty, *op. cit.*, p. 395; Johannes Messner, *Etica social, politica y economica a la luz del derecho natural* (Madrid: Rialp, 1967), pp. 1003-04.

[56] Pope Pius XII, *Discorsi e Radiomessaggi*, December 24, 1948, Vol. X, pp. 321-22.

[57] Vatican Ecumenical Council II, n. 81; *Catechismo della Chiesa Cattolica*, n. 2308.

[58] *Catechismo della Chiesa Cattolica* (Vatican City: Libreria Editrice Vaticana, 1997 —*editio typica*), n. 2302-2317.

[59] Welty, *op. cit.*, p. 383.

[60] *Ibid.*, p. 401.

[61] *Catechismo della Chiesa Cattolica*, 1992, n. 2309.

[62] Vatican Ecumenical Council II, n. 79; *Catechismo della Chiesa Cattolica*, 1992, n. 2312.

[63] *Ibid.*, n. 2313.

[64] Pope Pius XII, *Discorsi e Radiomessaggi*, October 19, 1953, vol.XV, p. 422.

[65] *Ibid.*, September 30, 1954, vol. XVI, p. 169.

[66] Messner, *op. cit.*, pp. 1005-06.

[67] *Ibid.*, p. 777-80; Welty, *op. cit.*, p. 388.

[68] Massimo de Leonardis, *Europa – Stati Uniti: un Atlantico più largo?* (Milan: Franco Angeli, 2001), pp. 185-200.

[69] Pope John XXIII, *Pacem in terris* (Vatican, April 11, 1963), N. 75; Vatican Ecumenical Council II, *Gaudium et Spes.* (Vatican, December 7, 1965), n. 82.

[70] Pope Pius IX, *Sillabus Errorum* (Appendix to Encyclical *Quanta Cura*. Vatican, 1864), prop. LXII; Pope Pius XII, *Discorsi e Radiomessaggi*, December 24, 1948, vol. X, p. 322.

[71] Roberto de Mattei, *"La sovranità necessaria. Riflessioni sulla crisi dello Stato moderno"* (Rome: Il Minotauro, 2001), pp. 174–75.

[72] Among the first publications on the "asymmetrical" war, see also Martin Van Creveld, *The Transformation of War* (New York: The Free Press, 1991); William S. Lind, "Defending Western Culture," *Foreign Policy* 84 (Fall 1991).

[73] Roger Mucchielli, *La Subversion* (Paris: C.L.C., 1976 —nouv. ed. revue et mise au jour), pp. 26-35; on psychological warfare in the "hyper-mediatism" era, see François GERE, *La guerre psychologique* (Paris: Economica, 1997), pp. 301-406.

[74] Pope Pius XII, *Discorsi e Radiomessaggi*, December 24, 1941, Vol. IX, p. 351.

[75] *Ibid.*, October 20, 1939, *Summi Pontificatus*, Vol. III, pp. 435-67.

[76] Pope John Paul II, "Messaggio per la Giornata Mondiale della Pace – 1 January 1981" in *Messaggi di pace: I discorsi integrali per la Giornata Mondiale della Pace dal 1968 al 1999* (Cantalupa-Turin: Effatà editrice, 1999), p. 133.

[77] *Ibid.*, "Messaggio per la Giornata Mondiale della Pace-1 January 1982," p. 351.

[78] Romano Amerio, *Iota unum* (Milan–Naples: Ricciardi, 1985), p. 379.

[79] Antonio Messineo, "Guerra," *Enciclopedia Cattolica,* Vol VI (1952), col. 1238.

[80] Pope Pius XII, *Discorsi e Radiomessaggi*, December 24, 1948, vol. X, p. 322.

[81] Pope John Paul II, *Veritatis Splendor* (August 6, 1993) – Italian Translation in *Insegnamenti* (Vatican City: Libreria Editrice Vaticana, 1995), vol. XVI, 2, n. 71-83.

The Islamic Holy War

A Millennium of Wars After the Edict of Medina

The year 622 is a crucial one in the history of Islam. Emigrating from Mecca to Yathrib, Muhammad (570-c. 632) renamed the latter "Medina," the "city" par excellence, and dictated its constitution. In this document, known also as the Chart or the Edict of Medina,[1] Muhammad outlines the fundamental characteristics of Islam as a community of believers fighting for an aim that is religious and political at the same time: to force Allah's law on the whole world.[2]

"Islam," according to the Koran (3:19), means "submission"[3]; and anyone who follows a religion other than Islam will not be accepted by God (3:85). The *jihad* was thus born in Medina, and it is the obligation Muslims have to fight the infidels into submission (9:29). Starting from the battle of Badr, which took place in March 624 and saw the inhabitants of Mecca defeated, Muhammad divided mankind into two categories: believers and nonbelievers; Muslims and infidels. "It is from Medina that the warring fanfare, which will resonate throughout its history, sets out"[4]; and the Koran, besides being a religious and legal text, may be also read as a treatise on military conquest, analogous to those by Sun Tzu, Machiavelli, and Clausewitz.[5] A few years after Muhammad's death, Islam penetrated the Iranian Highlands; in 634, the Muslims defeated the Byzantines at the Yarmuck River, fighting their way to Syria and Palestine; two years later, it was Egypt's turn; and, in 711, they invaded Spain and arrived in France. The Christian territories in northern Africa and the Middle East were annexed one after the other and served as outposts for Muslim attacks on Europe. By the end of the eighth century, Islam had already extended its rule over an immense territory from the Atlantic Ocean to the delta of the Indus River, and the holy war had become an inseparable feature of Islamic life.

In the end, King Charles Martel halted the Muslims' expansion into the West at the battle of Poitiers in 733. A long struggle ensued in Spain, which would rage for eight centuries, and, at the same time, a new Islamic power emerged in the East. At first under the Seljuk sultans, and then under the Ottomans, the Turks created one of the most powerful Islamic empires in history. After Mohammed II conquered Constantinople in 1453 and with it the whole Eastern Christian Empire, Muslims went on to seize Belgrade in 1521, conquer Hungary in 1526, and push as far as the gates of Vienna in 1529, until finally, in 1571, they were stopped at Lepanto by the Christian Holy League endorsed by Pope St. Pius V.

"For almost a thousand years from the first Moorish landing in Spain to the second Turkish siege of Vienna in 1683, Europe was under constant threat from Islam."[6] This threat was not limited to Central and Eastern Europe. The Barbary[7] pirates, from their bases in Maghreb, attacked and plundered Mediterranean towns and villages. Estimates are that, by 1830, when the French occupation of Algeria finally ended piracy and, therefore, slavery, the religious orders of Trinitarians and Mercedarians had ransomed over one million slaves from the hands of Muslim pirates.[8]

The Awakening of Contemporary Islam: "Book and Sword"

After World War I, the dismemberment of the Ottoman Empire, which was sanctioned in Severs on August 10, 1920, seemed to have signified the final decline of Islam. Vast Muslim territories in Asia and Africa were under the control of European empires and, with the exception of Iran, which was prey to chaos, only some far-off regions retained some degree of independence and sovereignty. Furthermore, a secular Islamic republic, Turkey, had emerged from the peace treaties.

The plan to "secularize" Islam through Western perceptions, however, had been challenged since the 1920's by a movement whose aim was to return to the classical sources of Islamic theology, the Koran and the Sunna.

The establishment in Egypt of the Muslim Brotherhood (*al-Ikwhan al Muslimun*) by Hasan al-Banna (1906-49) in 1928, and the 1941 founding on the Indian subcontinent of the *Jama'a at-i Islami* by Abu Ala al-Mawdudi (1903-79), are at the roots of the major Islamic contemporary movements.[9] Hasan al-Banna and Mawdudi, whose works have been translated into dozens of languages, are the classical authors of the Sunnite Islamic movements[10] and have been followed by others such as Sayyd Qutb (1906-66). Their thought is of fundamental importance in order to understand the Islamic movements of the 1990's and the contemporary Islamic *jihad*.

The new Islamic movements combine diverse aspects : They are a political party, a religious congregation, and a social movement at the same time.[11] They recruit their senior personnel from among intellectuals and their social base from urbanized masses, and they aim to overthrow the dominant structures in the Islamic world — namely, in opposition to the *ulema* and their tangible privileges deriving from their compromising with the ruling powers.[12]

The strength of Islam today rests not only on its control over a large proportion of the planet's energy resources and the dynamics of the demographic growth of its populations but on the consistency of its doctrine, which Mawdudi describes as "an organic and universal ideology, a total and complete system ("*nizam kamil wa chamil*").[13]

Islam, Hasan al-Banna argues, is

faith and worship, fatherland and nationhood, religion and state, spiri-
tuality and action, book and sword. The noble Koran speaks of all this,
regards it as the substance and integral part of Islam and recommends to
accept it to the utter consequences.[14]

Analyzing the nature of the Koranic method, Sayyd Qutb claims that, in the
Koran, Allah wanted to lay the foundations

of a community, of a movement and of a faith. He wanted the community and the movement to be founded on faith and faith to grow together
with them. He wanted faith to be the actual reality of that community in
movement and the community's life to be the incarnation of faith.[15]

"The Koran Is Our Constitution"

The philosophy of Islam is conveyed by the Koran and the Sunna. The Koran,
divided into 114 chapters or *suras*, collects in written form the "revelations"
said to have been handed over by Allah to Muhammad through the Archangel
Gabriel. The Sunna collects information and examples set forth in the shape of *hadith*, also defined as "dictums and deeds of the prophet."[16] "The Sunnah together
with the Koran constitute the shari'a,"[17] the "Islamic '*Lex*' which must be obeyed
both from a religious and as well as a civic point of view."[18] The Islamic *sharia* is
the fundamental constitution of Muslims:

All what agrees with this constitution is valid, all what opposes it is null
and void and never existed, irrespective of the ages and evolution of
thought on the law. Since the "*sharia*" has come from God through his
prophet's mouth, for it to be enforced in every time and place, it must be
applied until it is cancelled or annulled."[19]

The *sharia*, whose origin is Allah himself, is the sole source of Islamic law. The
Christian Faith makes a distinction between revealed and natural law: The latter
is inscribed on each man's heart, and duties and rights flow from it. In Islam, on
the contrary, the only law is the one revealed by Allah, and there exist no concepts
of "person" and "nature." Whereas, in Christianity, there is a role for reason, and
it is clearly distinguished from faith, in Islam, faith is the only path to knowledge.
From this point of view, there is a similarity between the Islamic concept of the
precedence of faith over all else ("fideism") and the Lutheran/Calvinist one.

In Islam, religion and politics form a single and inseparable whole. The slogan
"The Koran is our constitution"[20] effectively expresses the intimate union between
politics and religion in Islam and stands in opposition to the Gospels' maxim,

"give to Caesar the things that are Caesar's, and to God the things that are God's," which has been described by Sheikh al–Maraghi, grand master of the University Mosque of al–Azhar, as having no point of contact with the principles of Islam.[21]

Well-known scholar Bernard Lewis remarked that "It is by now evident that in Islam there is no distinction between church and state"[22]; therefore, there are not two separate powers, but one. He states that "the dichotomy of *regnum* and *sacerdotium* so crucial in the history of Western Christendom, has no equivalent in Islam."[23]

Contrary to Christianity, where the spiritual sphere is clearly distinct from the temporal one, in Islam, as Louis Gardet points out, "faith is in its essence a value of political relevance."[24] Medieval classical theologians and jurists acknowledge the legitimacy of political order only to the extent that it is subject to religion. As the German missionary to Africa Josef Stamer has written, "Islam is simultaneously religion and state, submission to its sole God through clearly codified rites and, at the same time, organizational pattern for society as a whole. Both are revealed by God. The religious ideal can only be fully accomplished through the political ideal, the Islamic city."[25]

Among Muslims, power and law do not find their legitimacy in a nation, fatherland, or dynasty, but in religion. Muslim law is not based on the *jus soli* (right by soil) or *jus sanguinis* (right by blood), but on *jus religionis*. "Neither '*jus soli'*, nor '*jus sanguinis*': it is religion that constitutes citizenship."[26]

Religion is not only universal but central, in the sense that Islam prevails over any other element as the ultimate foundation for identity, allegiance, and authority. "For a great deal of the documented history of most of the Islamic world, in fact" — Lewis clarifies — "the fundamental and primary criterion of definition, both internally and externally, was not the country or the nation, neither race or class, but religion, and for Muslims this naturally meant Islam."[27] This concept, Lewis recalls, was expressed with exceptional vigor and clarity by a grand vizier of the Ottoman Empire in 1917: "the fatherland of a Muslim is the place where the holy law of Islam applies."[28]

The reference point for Muslims is the *Umma*, the worldwide Islamic community established by Muhammad that finds its foundations in the divine Book. The *Umma* is not a state or a nation or a people; it is not even a church, but rather a religious community, the universal kinship of the believers in the Koran which includes all the countries where sharia applies. "You," the Koran says, "are the best people for you have been raised for the benefit of mankind; you promote good, forbid evil and believe in Allah" (3:110).

Sharia's historic mission to dominate the world is entrusted to the power of the *Umma*. The binding element in the *Umma* is the fight against the common enemy, the "infidel": The fight to impose sharia on the world is the way to Islamic unification.

The Arab fatherland (*watan al-arabiyya*) of nationalist regimes is but a transitional form bound to be absorbed into the Islamic community (*Umma al-islamiyya*), which, Qutb remarks, has nothing to do with a nation, a people, or a race, but is made up of all believers, irrespective of their fatherland, race, or color.[29]

To join the *Umma*, it is sufficient to profess exclusive faith in Allah (*shahadah*) with the appropriate ritual formula in the Arabic language. This profession of faith in the uniqueness of God (*tawhid*) is the most important of Islam's "pillars" and at the heart of Koranic doctrine. Indeed, it constitutes the most radical denial of the Christian Trinitarian revelation.

An Egalitarian Religion

In Islam, not only does all authority come from God (as it does in the Christian conception), but there is no authority other than God's. In the Islamic vision of the world, there is no legitimate sovereignty (*hakimmiyya*) besides the divine one. The character of Islamic theocracy is radically egalitarian.[30] Hierarchies would deny the absolute sovereignty of God, before whom all are equal in their "nothingness." In this sense, Islam can be described as a community dominated by the idea of perfect equality among believers (adult Muslim men only, that is). The imams, who do not actually constitute a clergy, are deprived of a real sovereignty: They are "wise" men trained at the most important religious schools, whose duty it is to perform many functions: as imams of big mosques; judges (*qazi*) in religious courts; legal experts who deliver pronouncements (*fatwa*) on legal or moral issues; etc.[31] "There is no priesthood in Islam and therefore no priestly mediation between God and the believer, no ordination, no sacraments and no rituals that only an ordained clergy can perform."[32]

Islamic theology denies the possibility that God's authority could be delegated to men, because of the unbridgeable gap separating divine omnipotence from any kind of human power. In fact, Islam is not familiar with the concept of participation, nor the Christian distinction between legitimate authority and abused power. "God rules alone, infinitely alone, in his inaccessible transcendence."[33] All that exists, including what is unjust, is motivated by God's will, for what God does not want cannot exist. Any authority, for Islam, is in a certain sense illegitimate, because only God has true legitimacy. By its own nature, human power is transitory and precarious, "just a machine at the service of believers' obligations,"[34] as sociologist Renzo Guolo notes. In this sense, he adds, "the fundamental feature of the Islamic political culture is the opposition between the concept of men's power-might and that of God's power-authority."[35]

The believer "is just a creature, a subject, a servant whose task is essentially that of following what the one Lord has ordered"[36] and, thus, to bring mankind back to absolute submission to the divine sovereignty over the world (*rububiyya*). For this task to be accomplished, Muslims ought to be entrusted with the guidance of all human societies. "Islam's ambition of worldwide expansion," Guolo remarks, "rests entirely on this very principle."[37]

The Muslim Brotherhood's theorist Sayyd Qutb proclaims that this perspective is

> a declaration of total war against any human power, in whatever form it presents itself and whatever kind of regulations it adopts, an all-out conflict wherever there are men claiming power, in one way or another, and therefore where in one way or the other idolatry is practiced. As a matter of fact, every system in which final decisions are entrusted to human beings and in which the source of every authority is human is a form of idolatry because it appoints some as Rulers of others in lieu of God.[38]

Jihad: *Islam's "Holy War"*

From an etymological point of view, the word *jihad* comes from the Arab root *jhd*, which means "effort," intended in the first place to accomplish God's will.[39] From a juridical point of view, though, the *Encyclopédie de l'Islam* clarifies that, "according to the classical doctrine and the historic tradition, jihad is the armed action taken in view of Islam's expansion and possibly of its defense."[40] It is indeed true that other terms, besides *jihad*, indicate the battle, in particular those deriving from the linguistic root of *qlt* or *hrb*.[41] But the term *jihad* is different from war; there can be secular wars, but only the *jihad* is "holy" because it refers to Islam's expansion all over the world through the use of arms.[42] The distinction between the interior *jihad* meant as the fight a Muslim wages against his own vices and passions, and the external *jihad*, which is precisely what a "holy war" consists of, is not an Islamic tradition but the product of a kind of agnostic — exoteric philosophy that aims at the "transcendental unity of all religions." The passage of the "*sura* of conversion" (Koran 9:29) defines *jihad* in the following terms:

> Fight those from among the People of the Book who believe not in Allah, nor in the Last Day, nor hold as unlawful that which Allah and His Messenger have declared to be unlawful nor follow the true religion, and who have not yet made peace with you, until they pay the tax willingly and make their submission.

And the eighth surah, verses 56-60, reads:

> worse than the beasts, in the sight of Allah, are those who have rejected the Signs of Allah and do not believe; those with whom thou makest a covenant every time and are not mindful of their obligation to Allah. When thou gainest mastery over them in war, then deal with them in such manner that those making hostile preparations beyond them should abandon their designs and be admonished. Shouldst thou apprehend treachery from a people who have made a pact with thee, terminate the pact in a manner that should occasion no prejudice to either side. Surely,

Allah loves not the treacherous. Let not the disbelievers imagine that they will gain any advantage over the believers through their machinations. Surely, they can never reduce the believers to helplessness. Make ready for them whatever you can of armed strength and of mounted pickets at the frontier, whereby you may daunt the enemy of Allah and your enemy and others beyond them whom you know not, but whom Allah knows. Whatever you spend in the way of Allah, it shall be repaid to you in full and you shall not be wronged.

"The jihad is an obligation. This precept is proclaimed in all the sources," the *Encyclopédie de l'Islam* reads.[43] The obligation lasts until the universality of Islam is accomplished. "Peace with non-Muslim nations is therefore temporary; and merely accidental circumstances may warrant it for a limited time only."[44]

He who complies with the obligation of the *jihad* is called *mujahid*. This obligation, imposed by God on all Muslims, knows no limit of time and place and must last until the whole world has accepted the Islamic faith or at least submitted to the Islamic power.

Until that happens, the world is divided into two: the House of Islam ("*dar al-Islam*"), where Muslims rule and the law of Islam prevails; and the House of War ("*dar al-Harb*"), comprising the rest of the world. Between the two there is a morally necessary, legally and religiously obligatory state of war, until the final and inevitable triumph of Islam over all non-believers.[45]

The *jihad* must be fought "for religious reasons," hence the importance of *fatawa,*, the legal pronouncements that legitimize or delegitimize a war.[46] "Holy war" has mainly an offensive connotation, for it presumes a permanent state of conflict between *dar al-Islam* and *dar al-Harb* that will end only when the whole world is finally submitted to Islam. The idea that *jihad* is a merely defensive war is denied by the very doctrine and tradition of Islam. Says Qutb:

He who therefore grasps the real nature of this religion . . . will realize the absolute necessity for the Islamic movement to embrace also the armed struggle ("*al-jihad bi-l-saif*"), alongside the commitment to preaching, and that this must not be intended as a defensive action, in the specific sense of defensive war, as the defeatists would wish who speak under the pressure of present circumstances or attacks by some shrewd orientalists. On the contrary, it is a momentum and a thrust for the liberation of man on this earth, resorting to all adequate means and the latest inventions in each era.[47]

Qutb's interpretation of *jihad* has deep roots; it is founded on the work of Ibn

Taymiya, a jurist of the 13th century. Furthermore, the ideologue of the qutbist group *al–Jihad*, which theorizes political assassination (*qatl*), Salam Faray, criticizes those doctors of the law, the so-called *Ulema*, who have deliberately forgotten for reasons of personal gain the duty of Muslims to rebel against the unholy power.[48]

The Two Parties: Islam and "Infidels"

> In the Muslim world view the first division of mankind is into the House of Islam and the House of War. The one consists of all those countries where the law of Islam prevails that is to say, broadly, the Muslim Empire; the latter is the rest of the world. Between the House of Islam and the House of War there is a state of war religiously and legally obligatory which could end only with the conversion or subjugation of all mankind[49].

The relation between the two houses is one of uninterrupted war, which is enforced by religious law; any truce is a purely matter-of-fact and temporary occurrence, since the Islamic strategy cannot be anything but war until the infidels are completely subjugated.[50]

In the Koran, each armed conflict stems from the fight of "believers" against "non-believers": "Fight in the cause of Allah against those who fight against you . . . kill them wherever you meet them, and drive them out from where they have driven you out" (2:190-191). And again, "kill [the idolaters] wherever you find them and make them prisoners and beleaguer them, and lie in wait for them at every place of ambush" (9:5); "then sue not for peace because of your slackness; for you will certainly have the upper hand" (47:35). "[T]he appropriate penalty for those who wage war against Allah and His Messenger and run about in the land creating disorder is that they be slain or crucified or their hands and their feet be cut off on alternate sides, or they be expelled from the land. That would be a disgrace for them in this world, and in the Here-after they shall have a great punishment" (5:33).

The "infidel" part of mankind is destined either to convert or to submit to Islam. To reach either goal is a sacred duty for all Muslims. All national, cultural, and class differences are absorbed into the only two important distinctions: that of faith (the "party of God") and that of error (the "party of Satan").[51]

Historically, the House of War *par excellence* has been Christendom, recently identified with the more general concept of "the West."[52] The West is the "great Satan" who confronts Islam in its struggle for world leadership. "The medieval definition itself of the crusading West, which re-evokes the Christian holy wars against Muslims and the symbolism connected to them, perfectly embodies this antagonist vision of the world."[53]

Westerners even today are known as *Ifrang* — i.e., "Franks," the Muslim name for the Crusaders; this term, together with the ancient definition of *bilal al-agam*, land of the barbarians, indicates Europeans and Europe or, more generally, anyone who comes from the West.[54] If the main adversary has always been Christendom and the West in general, the enemy *par excellence"* has changed from time to time according to who was the leading power in the Western world: starting from the Byzantine emperors to the rulers of the Western Roman Empire, followed by the European colonial powers and the United States of America.[55]

Today, the conflict between Islam and the West converges with the clash between the South and the North of the world, thus adding the dichotomy between oppressed and oppressor to the theological one between faithful and infidel in order to rally, alongside Muslims, neo-Marxists and upholders of "liberation theology" in an anti-Western appeal to all the "outcasts" of the Earth.

Some Muslims (for instance, Qutb), widen the traditional dichotomy between *Dar al-Islam* and *Dar al-Harb* to cover the one between *Dar al-Islam* and *jahiliyya*. The latter term, once used to signify pre-Islamic "barbarity,"[56] in the mouths of radical Islamists today indicates the corrupt and decadent West that, thanks to its penetration into the Islamic world, has now become an internal enemy of Islam.[57] Qutb says that, outside the *Umma* or community of believers, there is only the party of *jahiliyya*, consisting of "human demons, Crusaders, Zionists, idolaters, Communists who join forces whenever there is a sign of movements for the Islamic renaissance on earth to be destroyed and nullified."[58]

The international Western law, which behind its mask of universality promotes the interests of the Christian West, is regarded as incompatible with the "international Muslim law," based solely on the primacy of *sharia*, the "Law of God." Similarly. the modern concept of democracy is seen as incompatible with *sharia* and with the principle of the unity of God, which confers to Him, and not to people, the exclusive right to govern.[59] In fact, democracy is nothing less than polytheism, for it deprives Allah of the right to legislate and gives it to the people, thus expressing a secularized political vision poles apart from that of Islam.

Contrary to Christian doctrine and Western tradition, in the Muslim way of thinking, the practice of war is not in any way limited by precise moral rules that restrain its ferocity. For example, Islam does not acknowledge any legal rights of either non-Muslim persons or non-Muslim states, for the simple reason that it does not admit natural law or people's rights apart from *sharia*. "No believer ever dare bring aid to the misbeliever," a *hadith* proclaims.[60] With this in mind, enemies, once they fall prisoners, become "property" of the winners, who can free them or enslave them or even kill them: "when you meet in battle those who have disbelieved, smite their necks; and after the slaughter fasten tight the bonds, until the war lays aside its burdens. Then either release them as a favor, or in return for ransom" (Koran, 47:4). Terrorism is not prohibited by any precepts of the *Sunna* or Koran.

The Nature of Tolerance in Islam

In territories conquered by Islam, the only options left to the vanquished are conversion or death. Christians and Jews, as well as Sabeans and Zoroastrians, are defined as "people of the Book" or "people of the Pact" and enjoy a privileged if inferior status, so long as they subject themselves to Islam.[61] This legal status, called *dhimma*, includes the payment of a personal tax as public recognition of a person's subordination to Islam.

The pact of 'Umar, first successor to Muhammad, introduced badges for the protected — brown for the Mazdeists, blue for the Christians, yellow for the Jews — and confined the *dhimmi* in a particular neighborhood, which laid the foundations for the concept of the ghetto.[62]

The *dhimmi*, in consideration of the fact that they agree to subject themselves to Islam, are integrated into the Islamic community, but on heavy conditions of legal submission. They are excluded from public office and obliged to follow the social imperatives of *sharia*; religious proselytizing is punishable by death,[63] but the *dhimmi* must accept proselytizing by Muslims, even in their own churches and synagogues. Furthermore, the *dhimmi* may not erect anything higher than a Muslim construction; must bury their dead by stealth, without weeping; and are not allowed to ring bells, exhibit any object of worship, or proclaim their beliefs before a Muslim.[64] A Muslim man may marry a *dhimmi* woman, but a *dhimmi* man is not allowed to marry a Muslim woman, and a child born of a mixed marriage is always Muslim.[65] The punishment meted out to a Muslim murderer is reduced if the victim is a *dhimmi*.[66] Moreover, non-Muslims may never give evidence against a Muslim. Their oath is untrustworthy, according to the *hadith*,, given the perverse and lying nature of the "infidel" who persists in denying the superiority of Islam.[67] For the same reason, a Muslim, even if guilty, may not be sentenced to death if accused by an "infidel." On the contrary, it has happened at times that a *dhimmi* is put to death in lieu of a guilty Muslim.[68] A *dhimmi*'s inability to be a legal witness is particularly serious when he is accused of "blasphemy" against Muhammad, which is a capital offense.[69] Unable to contradict Muslim witnesses in court, such a person is often left with no option other than converting to Islam to save his life.[70]

The payment of the tax to which the *dhimmi* are subject, the *kharadj*, is justified on the grounds that territories taken from "infidels" belong by right to the Muslim community. According to this principle, each owner is but a mere tributary who keeps his land only by concession from the *Umma*, and this tax becomes the sacred symbol of an inalienable right granted by Allah to the winners on enemy soil.[71] In addition, the *dhimmi* must pay another tax, the *djizya*, which is imposed during a humiliating ceremony in which the *dhimmi* is beaten on the head or the nape of the neck.[72] Such is the nature of tolerance in Islam.

Jihad: A Problem of Authority

In the Islam of the "awakening," *jihad*, though newly popularized as a catch-phrase, is undermined by a deep-seated contradiction: the definition of the authority that should proclaim it.

The last public appeal to jihad in the 20th century was used by the Ottoman Empire against France, Great Britain, and Russia in order to justify its entering World War I on November 11, 1914. The Ottoman sultans sought to exert a political authority in the Islamic world that nobody today can duly claim: that of the khalif.

On the very evening of the death of the "Prophet," after many hours of violent discussions, the opinion prevailed that Muslims should retain political unity. Abu Bakr was elected as their leader, ostensibly the first to be given the title of khalif, an Arab word meaning both "successor" in a public office and "representative" or "vicar" of a superior authority.[73] The khalif is not a spiritual authority but a secular leader. He possesses an unlimited executive and judicial power but has no legislative power, since Islam does not know "legislators" but only "interpreters" of the only possible law, *sharia*.[74] The Islamic religion has no "supreme leader": Religious unity is maintained by the *Ulema*, whose task it is to see that Islamic doctrine is unaltered. The *Ulemas*, or doctors, are not an official corps but independent scholars, to whom public fame, not an established authority, confers the title of doctor.

The khalif may therefore be considered as a "Prince of Believers," whose mission is to preserve, with force if necessary, the territorial unity of the *Umma*, whose religious unity is in turn upheld by the *Ulema*.

To become khalif, one has to be Muslim, free, and a descendant of the Quraysh tribe. The khaliffate, nominally elective, became *de facto* hereditary after Muhammad's death, in the dynasty of Omayyadis (661-750) and in that of Abbasids (750-1258). The institution disappeared in 1258, when the Tartars conquered Baghdad and ended the Abbasids dynasty, but was subsequently reclaimed by Ottoman sultans who, from the end of the 18th century, have proclaimed themselves to be the supreme magistrates in Islam.

Following the fall of the Ottoman Empire in 1918, Kemal Ataturk, founder of the republic of modern Turkey, abolished the khaliffate, the only institution that to some extent symbolized the religious and political unity of Islam,[75] in November 1924. This act, "the most radically revolutionary ever recorded in the political history of the Muslim world,"[76] was born of the Turkish intelligentsia of the first postwar period, which saw the salvation of the nation in the separation of religion from the state. This was interpreted as a separation of the Turkish Republic from the rest of the Muslim world, and it sparked wide internal debate on the subject of supreme magistrates in Islam.

The radical Muslim and Pakistani ideologue Mawdudi has again proposed the khaliffate as the organizational core of *Umma*: "The just and equitable government is that which is based on the law which God has revealed through his prophets, and its name is Khaliffate."[77] If there is no khalif, there is no *auctoritas principis* who may legitimately proclaim *jihad* on behalf of the whole *Umma*. Nevertheless, *jihad* continues to be a collective and individual obligation for all Muslims.

Does Moderate Islam Exist?

I slamic doctrine is not as fully articulated as Western thinking is. Islamic thought is reduced to the dictates of a religion that places a believer in drastic "submission" to Allah.

The so-called five pillars of Islam[78] are purely superficial and boil down to the profession of a radical monotheism and the fight against any form of "polytheism," starting with the Christian Trinity, which constitutes the real antithesis to the Koran. The theological core of this conception is the "holy war." *Jihad* is essential to Islam, a religion that can be described in terms of "will to power" for the dynamic character of its divinity: pure will without the quality of a being.

War, revenge, and extermination feature prominently in the Koran, while no verses urge the believer to respect another's life. Holy war is a permanent state of conflict; truce, a temporary condition. Moderates and radicals alike share the idea that the whole of mankind will either convert to Islam or end up subject to its domination. To fight for this aim is the sacred duty of the Islamic community. In a word, Islam is conquest, and the only real distinction acceptable within it is that among strategies of conquest.

There can be (and, as a matter of fact, there is) discussion about the means, but the final objective of Islam is set: the extension of Koranic law to the whole world. The slogan of the Muslim Brotherhood — "God is our program, the Koran is our constitution, the Prophet our leader, the fight our path, the death for the glory of God the greatest of our aspirations" — encapsulates the common goals of this religion.[79]

It is not possible to understand Islam within the categories of modern Western thinking, imbued as they are with preconceptions from the Enlightenment. The distinction between "fundamentalism" and "progressivism" is part of a cultural legacy that is not applicable to the Muslim world,[80] so much so that it sees the process of modern secularization as a progress for mankind utterly incompatible with the principles of the Koran.

Current progressive language defines a "moderate" Muslim as one who recognizes the principles of secularism and tolerance and adjusts to the Western lifestyle: in a word, a Muslim who is not such, because he has abandoned the basic principles of his creed, or adheres to them only tepidly. In Islamic countries and in most Islamic communities in Europe, on the other hand, a "moderate" is simply one who rejects violence and particularly terrorism as a tool for the dissemination of Islam and the defense of the Islamic community. This does not mean that he considers his values compatible with those of the West.[81]

The "moderates" want to conquer Europe not by means of terrorist attacks but by means of demographic pressure, Islamicization of social structures, and the introduction of Islamic law into Western institutions. This soft, bottom-up strategy (which, according to the formula of Algerian president Boumedienne, aims to conquer the West through "woman's womb"), is counterbalanced by the harder, top-down strategy of "radical" Islam, which seeks to speed up the process by war and terrorism.[82]

Islamic discussion of the use of terrorism is not focused on any ethical judgment of the violence but on its consequences. "Moderates" contend that it might cause isolation and defeat, while radicals argue that it would bring victory. In any case, terrorism, as practiced both in Muslim countries against "apostates" as well as in the West against "infidels," complies with the Koranic principle of the *jihad*, just as the persecutions and massacres of Christians and other non-Muslims in Sudan, Pakistan, Bangladesh, and Indonesia do.[83] If the two camps differ in their strategy, they do not differ in their aim and are either focused on the Islamicization of everyday life and the conquest of territory or on political and military action, advocating *jihad* as a way to weed out and exterminate the enemy.[84]

The main promoters of the present-day "re-Islamicization" are not radical Islamist groups, but moderate Muslims who want to conquer European territory. The Arab League, founded in 1962 by Saudi Arabia, notwithstanding that country's strategic ties to the West, is the most active international instrument working for the diffusion of Islam in Europe. Its actions are today the major hurdle to the integration of Muslims into Western society.[85] In the West, the proliferation of mosques, the creation of financial networks, and the control of newspapers and TV networks are, for the most part, being funded by Saudi Arabia and the Arab league.[86]

Statistics speak loudly: Islam, which today is the second-largest religion on Earth with over one billion followers, is poised to become the second-largest national religion in many European countries. It is difficult to quantify this presence in Europe, but adding up legal and illegal immigrants, 20 million is a realistic number. Most of them come from the Maghreb (Spain and France) and Turkey (Austria and Germany). Their presence is mostly concentrated in cities, from London to Rome, from Marseilles to Frankfort, and it is made evident by the thousand mosques that are scattered throughout Europe, from Palermo to Stockholm: As recently as the 1970's, there were only 50 or 60 of them in total.[87] The mosque is not only a place to pray but a public and social space, a center for political and cultural propaganda—a reflection of the total vision of Islam, which ignores the Western distinction between the spiritual order and the civil and social dimension. "Moreover, it visibly marks the Islamicization of the territory, contributing to the reclaiming of the Islamic space which thus underlines its dissimilarity from the 'corrupt city' full of western symbols."[88] It bears repeating that Muslims are aggressively proselytizing in Europe but punish with the death penalty any similar efforts made by Christians in Islamic countries from Saudi Arabia to Sudan, from Pakistan to Indonesia.

A Clash of Civilizations

Islam may appear as a complex and protean reality lacking an institutionalized core, but beyond the ancient religious divisions (such as those between Sunnis and Shiites) and the new ones (more often than not political and strategic in nature), the Koran remains the one single reference point just as the goal remains one: namely, the conquest of the world, according to the words of the Prophet that state that "the whole earth is a mosque." Irrespective of its several doctrines, movements, organizations or peoples, Islam is in fact one single community of believers, the *Umma*, subject to one single law, the *sharia*.

"The *Umma* of the Muslims is the final stage of humanity since it is the authentic community of the elect people," remarks Guolo.[89] "The pan-Islamism of the *Umma*, in its radical version, closes the circle of the jihad's offensive vision."[90]

There are countries that accept Western secularization and others, such as Saudi Arabia, that seek to separate the West's technology from its culture. However, as Bernard Lewis notes, "in most Muslim countries Islam still remains the supreme yardstick of group identity and allegiance. It's Islam which makes for one's ego to be distinguished from the other."[91]

The "other" *par excellence* is nowadays represented by the West, which means Europe and the United States. For Muslims, the West is not only a theological mistake but a corrupt and degrading reality, responsible for the moral degeneration of the whole world.

The incompatibility of Islam and the West, this clash of civilizations, is rooted, even more than in the obvious religious differences, in the fact that Islam lacks any distinction between the political and religious spheres.

The propelling force behind this clash, as rightly pointed out by Samuel Huntington, does not lie in "fundamentalism" but in the very nature of Islam.[92] Islam, which does not forget and whose justice is an eye for eye and a tooth for a tooth, regrets the loss of Cordoba, Granada, and Palermo and does not forgive Europe for having dominated Islamic nations for centuries.[93]

The core doctrine of both traditional and contemporary Islam is that of *jihad*,[94] which, says Guolo, "manifests itself as a pure form of the new religious civil world war, which holds in radical Islam its warring party."[95]

While the West debates modern *versus* postmodern, Muslims do not plan to "modernize" Islam but to overcome the West and "Islamicize" modernity.[96] By the same token, the West must not be confused with its modernization, nor with consumer society, which is saturated with neopaganism. The peculiar features of the West, remarks Huntington, already existed considerably before its modernization: "The West was the West long before it was modern. The central characteristics of the West, those which distinguish it from other civilizations, outdate the modernization of the West."[97]

We must face the fact that the Islamic vision of the world is not only opposed to our secularized and modern world, but even more so to the traditional Christian society of the West. Islam is antimodern also in its most Westernized variety, such as Saudi Arabia's, and even in its most secularized variety, such as Iraq's, but, above all, is always and utterly radically anti-Christian. Before it was anti-Western and antimodern, Islam was anti-Christian. In the clash of civilizations that is ushering in the 21st century, the challenge of Islam is first of all a cultural and moral one. The West, which, in the course of its history, defined itself in part by defending itself against Islam, is today doomed to defeat if it deludes itself into opposing Muslims with the ideology of secularization. The only form of civilization that can prevail over Islam is unquestionably the Christian one.

Endnotes

[1] See Antonio D'Emilia, "Editto di Medina," *Novissimo Digesto Italiano*, UTET (Turin, 1964), vol.VI, pp. 404-05; integral text to be found in Montgomery Watt, *Islamic Political Thought* (Edinburgh: Edinburgh University Press, 1980), pp. 130-34.

[2] On the genesis of Islamic expansion, see Sergio Noja, *Maometto* (Fossano: Editrice Esperienze, 1974), pp. 199-219; Paolo Branca, *Introduzione all'Islam* (Cinisello Balsamo: San Paolo, 1995), pp. 49-54; WATT, *Islamic Political Thought*, pp.1-33.

[3] Sachiko Murata and William C Chittick, *The Vision of Islam* (St. Paul, Minnesota: Paragon House, 1994), pp. 3-7.

[4] Ignaz Goldziher, *Le dogme et la loi de l'Islam* (Paris: P. Geuthner , 1920), p. 7.

[5] Guillaume Faye, *La colonisation de l'Europe. Discours vrai sur l'immigration et l'Islam* (Paris: L'Encre, 2000), p. 121.

[6] Bernard Lewis, *Islam and the West* (New York: Oxford University Press, 1993), p. 13 .

[7] Jacques Heers, *Les Barbaresques. La corse et la guerre en Méditerranée, XIV–XVI siécles* (Paris: Perrin, 2001).

[8] Rinaldo Panetta, *I saraceni in Italia* (Milan: Mursia, 1998), p. 286.

[9] On contemporary Islam, see Richard P. Mitchell, *The Society of Muslim Brothers* (Oxford: Oxford University Press, 1969); Olivier Carré, *L'Islam et l'Etat dans le monde aujourd'hui* (Paris: PUF, 1982); Bruno Etienne, *L'Islamismo radicale* (Milan: Rizzoli, 1988); Renzo Guolo, *Il partito di Dio. L'Islam radicale contro l'Occidente* (Milan: Guerini e Associati, 1994); Renzo Guolo, *Avanguardia della fede. L'Islamismo tra ideologia e politica* (Milan: Guerini e Associati, 1999).

[10] Olivier Roy, *Généalogie de l'Islamisme* (Paris: Hachette, 1995), p. 35.

[11] *Ibid.*, p. 45.

[12] Valeria Fiorani Piacentini, "Il pensiero militare nel mondo islamico," vol. I, "Credenti e non credenti: il pensiero militare e la dottrina del jihad," *Rivista Militare* (1991): 235; Roy, *op. cit.*, p. 41.

[13] Guolo. *Il partito di Dio*, p. 56.

[14] Paolo Branca, *Voci dell'Islam moderno. Il pensiero arabo-mussulmano fra rinnovamento e tradizione* (Genoa: Marietti, 1997), p. 194.

[15] *Ibid.*, p. 196.

[16] Al-Bukhari, *Detti e Fatti del Profeta dell' Islam* (Turin: Utet, 1982).

[17] S.A.A. Mawdudi, *The Islamic Law and Constitution* (Lahore: Islamic Publications Ltd, 1975), p. 69.

[18] Antonio D'Emilia, *Scritti di diritto islamico*, collated by Francesco Castro (Rome: Istituto per l'Oriente, 1976), p. 47.

[19] Uda Abd Al-Qadir, "La sharia: costituzione fondamentale dei musulmani" in *Dibattito sull'applicazione della sharia* (Turin: Edizioni della Fondazione Giovanni Agnelli, 1995), p. 15.

[20] Renzo Guolo, *Il partito di Dio*, p. 30.

[21] Louis Gardet, *La Cité Musulmane. Vie sociale et politique* (Paris: Vrin, 1981, enhanced edition), p. 25.

[22] Bernard Lewis, *La rinascita islamica* (Bologna: Il Mulino, 1991), Italian translation, p. 281.

[23] Bernard Lewis, *The Crisis of Islam: Holy War and Unholy Terror* (New York: Random House, 2003), p. 6.

[24] Gardet, *op. cit.*, p. 25.

[25] M. Josef Stamer, *L'Islam en Afrique au sud du Sahara* (Koeningstein: Aide à l'Eglise en Détresse, 1995), p. 11.

[26] Gardet, *op. cit.*, p. 27; Lewis, *La rinascita islamica*, p. 280; J. Vatikiotis Panayotis, *Islam: stati senza nazioni* (Milan: Il Saggiatore, 1993), Italian translation, p. 47.

[27] Lewis, *La rinascita islamica*, p. 341.

[28] *Ibid.*, p. 300.

[29] Renzo Guolo, *Il partito di Dio*, p. 73.

[30] Stefano Nitoglia, *Islam, Anatomia di una setta* (Milan: Effedieffe, 1994), pp. 47-49.

[31] Roy, *op. cit.*, p. 25.

[32] Lewis, *The Crisis of Islam*, p. 9.

[33] Gardet, *op. cit.*, p. 35.

[34] Guolo, *Il partito di Dio*, p. 31.

[35] *Ibid.*, p. 32.

[36] Branca, *Voci dell'Islam moderno*, p. 207.

[37] Guolo, *Il partito di Dio*, p. 67.

[38] Quoted in Branca, *Voci dell'Islam moderno*, p. 198.

[39] Mehdi Abedi and Gary Legenhausen, *Jihad and Shahadat: Struggle and Martyrdom in Islam* (Houston, TX: IRIS, 1986), pp. 1-45.

[40] Halim Sabit Sibay, "Jihad" in *Encyclopédie de l'Islam*, Vol.II (1965), pp. 551-53.

[41] Giorgio Vercellin, *L'Islam e la guerra* (Florence: Giunti, 1997), p. 53.

[42] Rudolph Peters, *Jihad in Classical and Modern Islam* (Princeton: Markus Wiener, 1996), pp. 1-7.

[43] Sibay, *op. cit.*, p. 551.

[44] *Ibid.*, p. 552.

[45] Bernard Lewis, *The Political Language of Islam* (Chicago: The University of Chicago Press, 1991), p. 85.

[46] Fiorani Piacentini, *op. cit.*, pp. 50-51.

[47] Quoted in Branca, *Voci dell'Islam moderno*, p. 199.

[48] Guolo, *Il partito di Dio*, pp. 41-42.

[49] Bernard Lewis, *The Muslim Discovery of Europe* (New York: Norton and Company, 1991), pp. 60-61.

[50] Vercellin, *op. cit.*, p. 41.

[51] Guolo, *Il partito di Dio*, p. 75.

[52] Lewis, *La rinascita islamica*, pp. 290-91.

[53] Guolo, *Avanguardia della fede*, p. 69.

[54] Guolo, *Il partito di Dio*, p. 82; Lewis, *The Muslim Discovery of Europe*, p. 135.

[55] Lewis, *La rinascita islamica*, p. 291.

[56] Ignaz Goldziher, *Muslim Studies* (London: George Allen & Unwin, 1967), vol. 1, pp. 201-07.

[57] Guolo, *Avanguardia della fede*.

[58] Quoted in Guolo, *Avanguardia della fede*, pp. 26-27, 67.

[59] Guolo, *Il partito di Dio*, p. 63.

[60] Sergio Noja, *Maometto profeta dell'Islam* (Milan: Mondatori, 1991), p. 176.

[61] Antoine Fattal, *Le Statut Lègal de non-musulmans en pays d'Islam* (Beirut: Imprimerie catholique, 1958), pp. 71-84, 234-36; Claude Cahen, "Dimma" in *Encyclopédie de l'Islam*, vol. II (1965), pp. 234-38; Chafik Cherata, "Dimma" in *Encyclopédie de l'Islam*, vol. II (1965), p. 238; Stefano Nitoglia, *op. cit.*, pp. 50-52; Giovanni Cantoni, *Aspetti in ombra della legge sociale dell'Islam. Per una critica della vulgata "islamicamente corretta"* (S. Cataldo, Caltanissetta: Centro Studi sulla Cooperazione "A. Cammarata," 2000), pp. 111-32.

[62] Guolo, *Il partito di Dio*, p. 99.

[63] Cahen, *op. cit.*, p. 235.

[64] Fattal, *op. cit.*, pp. 79, 82.

[65] *Ibid.*, pp. 79, 82.

[66] Bat Ye'or, *Juifs et Chrétiens sous l'Islam. Les dhimmis face au défi intègriste* (Paris: Berg International, 1994), p. 34.

[67] Nitoglia, *op. cit.*, p. 51.

[68] *Ibid.*

[69] Fattal, *op. cit.*, p. 77.

[70] Bat Ye'or, *op. cit.*, p. 33.

[71] Nitoglia, *op. cit.*, pp. 51-52.

[72] *Ibid.*, p. 52.

[73] Carlo Alfonso Nallino, *Raccolta di scritti editi e inediti. Vol. III: Storia dell'Arabia preislamica. Storia e instituzioni musulmane* (Rome: Istituto per l'Oriente, 1941), pp. 235-36; Watt, *Islamic Political Thought*, pp. 31-45.

[74] Nallino, *op. cit.*, p. 236.

[75] *Ibid.*, pp. 227–59.

[76] Ali Merad, *L'Islam Contemporain* (Paris: Presses Univesitaries de France, 1995), p. 77.

[77] Quoted in Branca, *Voci dell'Islam moderno*, p. 208.

[78] Nitoglia, *op. cit.*, p. 12; Montgomery Watt, *Breve storia dell'Islam* (Bologna: Il Mulino, 2001), Italian translation, pp. 65-72.

[79] Quoted in Guolo, *Avanguardia della fede*, p. 18.

[80] "It is now common usage to apply the term "fundamentalist" to a number of Islamic radical and militant groups. The use of this term is established and must be accepted, but it remains unfortunate and can be misleading." Lewis, *The Political Language*, pp. 117-18. See also Etienne, *op. cit.*, pp. 144-47; Branca, *Voci dell'Islam moderno*, p. 70; Watt, *Breve storia dell'Islam,* p. 119.

[81] Jean–Luc Giorda, "Ma esiste un Islam moderato?" *Il Tempo* (October 11, 2001).

[82] Guolo, *Avanguardia della fede*, pp. 55 -60.

[83] Alexandre Del Valle, *L'Islamisme et les Etats–Unis. Une alliance contre l'Europe* (Lausanne: L'Age d'Homme, 1997), p. 93.

[84] Guolo, *Avanguardia della fede*, p. 56.

[85] Roy, *op. cit.*, pp. 101, 107.

[86] Del Valle, *Guerres contre l'Europe*, pp. 101-05.

[87] Felice Dassetto and Alberto Bastenier, *Europa: Nuova frontiera dell'Islam* (Rome: Edizioni del Lavoro, 1991); Silvio Ferrari, *L'Islam in Europa. Lo statuto giuridico della comunità musulmana* (Bologna: Il Mulino, 1996).

[88] Guolo, *Avanguardia della fede*, pp. 58-59.

[89] Guolo, *Il partito di Dio*, p. 77.

[90] *Ibid.*, p. 75.

[91] Lewis, *La rinascita islamica*, p. 279.

[92] Huntington, *op. cit.*, pp. 286-87.

[93] Del Valle, *L'Islamisme et les Etats–Unis*, pp. 14-15.

[94] Fiorani Piacentini, *op. cit.*, p. 233.

[95] Guolo, *Avanguardia della fede*, p. 28.

[96] Roy, *op. cit.*, pp. 53, 62.

[97] Huntington, *op. cit.*, p. 69.

Crusade, *Jihad*, and Modern Tolerance

Holy War and Just War

S ome intellectuals like to draw a parallel between *jihad* and the type of Christian just war that we call *crusade*. They would lump both together into the same conceptual category: that of "war of religion."[1]

Such people advocate pacifism and tolerance in opposition to the "spirit of crusade," and their vision of the world, which goes to the extreme of denying legitimacy even to just war, dates as far back as certain late-medieval sects and to others of the 16th century, such as the Anabaptists, who paradoxically even promoted wars and revolutions to affirm their right not to bear arms.[2]

The parallel is superficial and shows a lack of understanding of both religions. By comparing the two forms of holy war, we will define the characteristics of the crusade, both as an historical institution and as a permanent category of the Christian spirit.

Instituit nostro tempore praelia sancta: "In our time, God has instituted holy wars," wrote Guibert, abbot of Nogent, in the early 12th century, in his Chronicle of the First Crusade, aptly named *Gesta Dei per Francos*.[3] The doctrine of crusade, seen as Christian "holy war," besides being found in the Old Testament, where wars are holy even down to such details as rites and practices,[4] goes back to the prototypical Christian warrior and crusader Charlemagne, and to the theory of war by Saint Augustine, which he developed well before the birth of Islam.[5]

Christian holy war must be distinguished from a just war that can be waged by a temporal sovereign to defend his state from an enemy. Erdmann points out that, in the widest sense of the term, *holy war* should denote only a war that is conceived as a religious act or is proclaimed by a spiritual authority who represents mostly religious interests.[6] If not every just war is holy, the holy war, in Christian thinking, is not only just but is the just war *par excellence*. Hence, "the Crusade was the perfect example of the just war, *'justissimum bellum,'* and the idea of a just war was inevitably developed and refined during the age of Crusades."[7]

The Christian distinction between holy war and just war, which in turn derives from the distinction between the spiritual authority and the temporal one, enables us to comprehend the basic differences between the crusade and the *jihad*, which I will now examine from both the legal-institutional outlook and its spiritual-inner side.

The Legal Dimension of the Crusade

Crusades differ from *jihad* in their juridical-institutional aspect—*i.e.*, in the authority that can legitimately proclaim a holy war. In the Christian view, which makes a distinction between the temporal and spiritual powers, temporal rulers may proclaim "just wars," but only the pope can declare a crusade. The power of co-action, *pleno jure*, both at spiritual and material levels, comes to the Church from the character of perfect society which is befitting to Her, and the Crusades are an historical expression of it.[8]

In his *Decretum*, Gratian writes that, "while clerics could not themselves bear arms, they could legitimately exhort ('*hortari*') others to defend the oppressed and attack the enemies of God"[9]: *Ad oppressorum defensionem, atque ad inimicorum Dei oppugnationem eis licet hortari*[10]. In support of this principle, the Bolognese jurist quotes a certain number of canons which show how the pope can give instructions for an army to be gathered against Saracens (canon 7) and must be the vindicator of his flock (canon 8). In fact, Pope "Leo IV, who in about 852 had called a force together to defend Rome against Saracen pirates, also saw himself as an avenger and defender of his flock."[11]

The ultimate symbol of the pope's intervention on the battlefields is the standard of the Church, *vexillum Sancti Petri*, which the pope hands over to those who fight in his name.[12] Pictured on the mosaic in the Lateran, Saint Peter can be seen bestowing the standard on Charlemagne. This gesture, frequently repeated in the second half of the 11th century, was one of the first ways the papacy used to consecrate a military expedition. The history of this standard culminated in the establishment of a papal office—namely, the "standard-bearer of the holy Roman Church," whose origin, notes Erdmann, is closely tied to the idea of crusade.[13]

The history of the Crusades is intimately connected to that of the papacy. In the 11th century, when Christendom was torn apart by discord and the Church was the supreme reference point, it was a pope, the blessed Urban II, who rallied the Christian princes under the same standard to stem the advancement of the Turks and free the Holy Land.[14] The bulls of crusades and canons of councils always present, as the main goal of a crusade, the retaking of the Holy Land or, according to the historical circumstances, the safeguarding of the Christian Kingdom of Jerusalem (the result of the First Crusade). These are eminently religious goals, which have their "ultimate motivation in the sacredness of the holy places, on which, after the birth, life and death of Jesus Christ, the Church has an unquestionable right."[15] Not only must the shrine of Christ be accessible to pilgrims, but infidels must not be allowed to insult the holy city by having a dominant presence there. The Holy Land is, in fact, "the legacy of Christ": It is the land on which Christ trod while on earth, the land of the people of Israel, whose legitimate inheritors through Christ are the Christians.

The Crusaders sing the words by Renaut de Beauvais: "Those who have been baptized / are the heirs of this land / where the Son of God wanted to suffer /

martyrdom and passion for us."[16]

An Army of Penitents and Pilgrims

Many 20th-century historians have highlighted the spiritual dimension of the Crusades. While they were a warring enterprise, they were at the same time also an extraordinary occasion for conversion, in the profound sense that the Middle Ages attributed to this term.

The prevailing sentiment that shaped the crusading spirit, according to Jean Richard, is the awareness of one's sin.[17] According to other scholars, the liberation of the holy shrine bears a theological significance in the sense that Christ, by His Death and Resurrection, freed man from death and sin once and for all.[18] The loss of the Holy Land is therefore seen as a result of men's sins, a punishment inflicted by God so that the guilt of humanity would appear more evident. The Council of Clermont had already decided that the pilgrimage to Jerusalem would have served as *pro omnia poenitentia*, and Urban II and his successors granted the remission of every sin and a plenary indulgence for all those who left for the Holy Land. The Crusaders marched as "armed pilgrims" to atone for their sins in a "noble pilgrimage which purifies the errant soul so that it can be offered immaculate and pristine to God."[19] In this sense, the crusading army, as pointed out by Paul Alphandéry in his well-known work on Christianity and the idea of crusade, was "an army of penitents" who sought, through this fight, to win eternal reward in heaven.[20] "The Crusade," writes Richard, "was an army of pilgrims, which, animated by a spirit of poverty and sacrifice, turned into an army of penitents."[21]

British historian Jonathan Riley-Smith devoted an interesting study to the crusade "as an act of love."[22] In his essay, he recalls the bull *Quantum praedecessores*, dated December 1, 1145, in which Pope Eugene III, referring to those who had responded to the appeal of the First Crusade, says that they were "inflamed by the ardour of charity."[23] Urban II and St. Bernard of Clairvaux also spoke of charity and the love of God as motivations for the Crusade. Love of God and love of one's neighbor are expressions of the same flame of charity: The crusade, writes Richard, "first of all accomplished the duty to assist brethren in danger, to which assistance to those in need is added. This love among Christians is the starting point of the Crusade, and was also the *'raison d'être'* of the religious orders brought into being by the Crusades, Templars and Hospitaliers."[24]

The "Armed Force" of the Church

The above considerations, while correct, must not overshadow the institutional aspect of the Crusades. They were not popular uprisings, "spontaneous" armed pilgrimages, but first and above all, as Cardinal Castillo Lara rightly underlines in his important volume on "ecclesiastical coaction," military expeditions promoted and directed by the Church.[25] If the Crusades were led and manned by laypeople (kings, princes, feudal lords and ordinary faithful), the remote but ultimate leader was none other than the pope, on whom the crusading armies directly depended, thus constituting the Church's army. Cardinal Castillo Lara summarizes the characteristics of these wars as follows[26]:

> 1) The pope himself promulgates the crusade, with a relevant bull, which promises indulgences and privileges.
>
> 2) The Church intervenes to all intents and purposes in recruiting the army, through preaching and the instrument of *votum crucis* (vow of the cross).
>
> 3) The pope establishes the moment of departure for the Crusaders, which is called, in canonic literature, *passagium generale* (general passage).
>
> 4) The Church actively participates in running military operations. Being unable to participate personally, the pontiffs are represented by legates who do not direct the war but perform an important advisory role.

To sum it up, the Church considered the crusading army as Her own army, whose supreme command belonged to the pope, who was in turn represented by a legate, who would accompany the troops and advise the military leaders in full agreement with the pontiff. The Church was aware that She was wielding her coactive power in the Crusades, the so-called *potestas gladii ecclesiastica*.

> In launching their appeal for the Crusades, in encouraging the soldiers by taking them under their high protection, the pontiffs never wondered whether war itself was inconsistent with the spirit of the Church, neither did they ask themselves whether they had the right to gather armies and pit them against the infidels. . . . [T]herefore not only did the Pontiffs not consider it illicit, but on the contrary, they were conscious of exerting their authority, namely the supreme power of material coaction; neither did they ever think to invade thus the temporal sphere, which they acknowledged was reserved only to the state.[27]

In this respect, the difference between the crusade and *jihad* is fundamental. The confusion that exists in Islam between the spiritual and temporal order does not permit it to distinguish between "just" wars that are not necessarily holy, and "holy" wars that have a spiritual object. The Islamic community is, at the same time, religious and political, and *jihad* is by definition always "holy," even when it is politically motivated. But Islam has no spiritual authority, similar to the pope, who could proclaim a *jihad*: It is up to ordinary lay people such as the *ulemas* to proclaim it. That means it is possible that "holy wars" could be proclaimed that conflict with one another, for in Islam there is no single and supreme source of spiritual authority other than the Koran.

While the khalif is a sort of monarch who acts as the military leader of a *jihad,* he may not proclaim it, because his is not a spiritual but a temporal authority. The *jihad* therefore is a war without an institutional dimension, substantially anarchical and egalitarian, in the sense that each Muslim is a *mujahideen* living in a permanent state of "holy war," whereas, in Christendom, the crusade is a particular public initiative that it is only and specifically up to the Church to proclaim.

The Inner Dimension of the Crusade

Alongside the institutional dimension, there is an inner dimension to the Crusade, a "spirit" that the modern mind-set can hardly understand, tending to interpret it as a cover-up for political and economic interests. Yet the Crusades were a collective enterprise of men from all walks of life and every corner of Europe; men who responded to the appeal by the papacy by turning their backs on the stability of their own lives; men who left their families, cities, and fiefs to venture on an unknown path, not out of personal interest, but to bear witness to their true and profound Faith, with the intention of liberating and defending the holy shrine from enemies who had raised the banner of the Crescent where Jesus Christ had raised His Cross and shed His Divine Blood.

These epic deeds are even today impressing historians for their nobility and generosity, and, by understanding them, we can better understand the inner and combative dimension of the Catholic religion, by comparing the ideal vision of the Crusades with the ideals of the enemy the Crusaders were facing.

The difference between *jihad* and crusade is ultimately rooted in the profound difference between the Christian God and Allah. Christendom is centered on the mystery of the Holy Trinity and the Word's Incarnation. Jesus Christ, true God and true Man, redeemed humanity from sin, opening up for us the gates of grace. This grace is the Holy Ghost, Third Person of the Holy Trinity, dwelling in the soul of the Christian, and the faith that the Holy Trinity awakens in the soul is a far cry from the humane religious sentiment of the Muslim.

Islamic monotheism has nothing to do with the Christian one but is, rather, its downright opposite.[28] Muslims are the first to acknowledge this, reciting with the Koran: "Those certainly are disbelievers who say: Allah is the third of three" (5:73). Not only is Allah not one-in-three, he is not a being or a person, either.[29] Allah is a will in action that demands submission.

"The living God is only one: if he is the one revealed by Jesus Christ he cannot be the one described by the Koran."[30] Islam is condemned to be a ritualized, exterior religion, because it is deprived of the supernatural influence of grace whose Source is the second Person of the Holy Trinity.

Unlike the Christian just war, *jihad* is an offensive war, a war of aggression, precisely because Islam, not experiencing the inner dimension of Christianity, can only expand by force. Allah does not love men and does not ask for their love; he simply demands their subjection.[31] His imperative is to submit the whole world to himself. The nonbelieving world has no right to exist, other than to choose between conversion and destruction.

To convert to Islam, in fact, calls for no more than a profession of monotheism and a series of formal rituals, the "five pillars of Islam," — namely, the pilgrimage to Mecca; fasting during Ramadan; charitable giving; ritual prayer; and the profession of monotheism. No one is asked to transform his soul or radically reorient his life.

Islamicist Sergio Noja recalls that, according to tradition, someone asked Muhammad, "If I perform the ritual prayer, pay my tax, do my Ramadan fasting and all the other legal acts and nothing else, will I enter Paradise?" Muhammad's answer was a simple "Yes." Noja comments that the "Christian answer would have been certainly different, and many Christians would surely accuse Mohammed's answer of being pharisaical."[32] Such pharisaical dimension is confirmed by the fact that Islam condones lying[33]; to be precise, it contemplates the possibility of outwardly denying one's faith, precisely because it does not demand a strict inner consistency between what one's mind thinks and what one's lips utter.

Christianity, on the other hand, is an inner religion that is fostered by the supernatural life of the human soul. Baptism is the sacrament which instills this supernatural life, the life of grace. Thanks to it, a person undergoes an inner transformation that finds its foundation in Jesus Christ, who says: "I am the vine, ye are the branches" (John 15:5).

Precisely because of this quality, Christianity is capable of profoundly transforming civilizations and mentalities, shaping societies from the inside and winning converts among pagan and barbarian people by persuasion rather than force. Civilizations, too, have lives and deaths and souls, to the extent that the truth of the Gospel changes their laws, institutions, and even their traditions and morals from the inside. This is exactly what happened with the birth and the advancement of the Christian Middle Ages.

The words of Jesus Christ, "Go ye into all the world, and preach the gospel to every creature. He that believeth and is baptized shall be saved; but he that believeth not shall be damned" (Mark 16:15-16), prompted the Apostles as well as their successors, the missionaries, to propagate the doctrine of truth into all corners of the world, appealing to human hearts with the instruments of the Word and the example of Christ.

The Christian conquest of many societies, which was initiated by the Apostles and the disciples of Jesus Christ, was not accomplished by force but peacefully, through the conquest of souls, minds, and hearts. Yet a society that had peacefully turned Christian constituted a *corpus* — that is, a community that was entitled to be defended, by force if necessary, from those who wanted to thwart the results of our Lord's Passion. In this sense, the Crusades can be described as just wars and, at the same time, in the words of the French scholar Flori, "holy war *'par excellence.'*"[34]

Flori has wisely noted that, between *jihad* and crusade, there is an essential difference in that "the first preaches the conquest, the second the re-conquest."[35] Nobody may be forced to believe, says Saint Augustine,[36] and the Church confirms this thinking by describing faith as a free act that cannot be imposed on an individual. Those who initiate a holy war, like the Crusaders, do not intend to impose their religion, but to defend it. "Christ's faithful," St. Thomas Aquinas explains, "often wage war with unbelievers, not indeed for the purpose of forcing them to believe . . . but in order to prevent them from hindering the faith of Christ."[37] To this purpose, Russell clarifies that "Pope Innocent IV denied that Christians could make war on Saracens merely because they were infidels, and expressly prohibited wars of conversion. But when Saracens invaded Christian territories and attacked Christians, both the Church and the Christian prince of the territory could wage a just war to avenge their injuries and losses."[38]

The Crusades began as an armed defense of the Christian civilization that had its origin in the peaceful conquest of hearts by missionaries thanks to what Saint Paul calls "the sword of the Spirit" (Ephesians 6:17). There is thus a similarity in the cross brandished by the missionaries and that raised by the Crusaders. Both embraced the very same cross, offering, according to their different vocations, battles and sacrifices for the same ideal.

The supreme aim of the missionaries was the *plantatio Ecclesiae*, the establishment of the Christian Church and way of life.[39] Pope Pius XII claims that

> the purpose of the Crusades was to liberate the Holy Land, and above
> all the Tomb of Christ, from the hands of the infidels: there is no doubt
> about this noble and lofty aim! Moreover they were necessary to defend
> the faith and Christian civilization in the west from Islam. This task did
> not end after the position of Christianity was stabilized. The aim was to
> make the whole world a Holy Land. The goal was to spread the king-
> dom of the Risen Redeemer, on whom all earthly and celestial power
> had been bestowed (Matthew 28:18), among the hearts of all men all over
> the world, reaching the humblest dwelling house and every single man
> who walked upon the earth.[40]

The Knight-Monks in the Age of the Crusades

Both the spiritual and institutional aspects of the Crusades were perfectly evident in the religious military orders, such as the Hospitallers of St. John (subsequently called "Rhodes Knights" and, to end with, "of Malta") and the Templar and Teutonic knights, which were born and developed during the Crusades and whose adherents combined, in the words of St. Bernard of Clairvaux, "the meekness of the monk and the courage of the warrior."[41] Cardinal Castillo Lara writes that

> Military orders are a faithful illustration of what could be regarded as the ecclesiastic "*vis armata*." In fact, its members were soldiers and monks at the same time. As religious men, they professed the three traditional vows on a rule approved by the Holy See. As soldiers, they formed a permanent army ready to engage in battle wherever there was a threat by enemies of the Christian religion. Their exclusive ecclesiastic aim and their dependence on the Holy See as a consequence of their obedience vow, made them soldiers of the Church.[42]

St. Bernard of Clairvaux addressed the budding order of the Templars in such a manner:

> The knights of Christ can fight the battles of Our Lord with a peaceful conscience, with no fear whatsoever either of committing sin by killing the enemy, or of the danger of death, for in this case death, inflicted or suffered for Christ, is by no means a crime and brings with it the merit of glory many times over. In fact, in the first instance one renders glory to Christ, while in the second instance one obtains Christ himself. Undoubtedly He willingly accepts an enemy's death as retribution; all the more willingly does He give himself to the soldier as consolation. The knight of Christ kills with an easy conscience and dies with even greater safety. By dying he benefits himself; by killing he benefits Christ. It's not without reason that the soldier carries his sword. He is a minister of God for the punishment of the wicked and the exaltation of the good. When he kills a wicked man, he is not a homicide, but rather a wickedcide, so it is necessary to see him both as the avenger serving Christ and the defender of the Christian people. When he subsequently dies, one ought not to think that he is dead, but that he has won eternal glory.[43]

With these words, the ideal of the Christian holy war reaches its culmination, and stands in utmost opposition to modern relativism, which makes the principle of tolerance a dogma.

The Modern Dogma of Tolerance

The main objection to the concept of either Christian or Islamic "holy war" is its incompatibility with the modern principle of tolerance — a principle so dearly held it has become in some circles a dogma. From the Christian perspective, however, tolerance is not and cannot be an ideological dogma, nor an ultimate end, but only a practical and prudential attitude of indulgence toward an opinion or a behavior that is considered unjust.[44]

Christian tolerance is mostly based on the moral virtue of prudence, that "with which we rightly judge—in each individual case—what ethics demands of us"[45]; but it is not a virtue in itself because virtues are immediate expressions of moral good, whereas tolerance is a response that entails good, without being in itself a good in the proper sense of the word. Tolerance may be just, but it may also be imprudent and wrong, so much so that in our everyday speech we may describe as "intolerable" something that we cannot accept or endure. On the other hand, when we talk of natural or supernatural virtues, the words we use always have an absolutely positive connotation. There cannot be an excess of charity or patience, and, if pushed to the extreme, such virtues only increase in strength and intensity, whereas extreme tolerance may turn into a fault or sin.

The concept of tolerance that was developed by religious sects in the 16th and 17th centuries and, later, by Locke, Voltaire, and Rousseau continues to this day and is very different from the Christian one. This tolerance is no longer a practical and prudential attitude, which still presupposes an ultimate truth, but an ideological dogma we can call *tolerantism,* which denies the existence of an identifiable truth and which means, in the end, sheer indifference to all.

This tolerantism is the source of pacifism, the doctrine that, under the pretext of exalting peace, condemns any use of force and any kind of killing, from the death penalty to war, even when the latter is nothing but a defensive war. Underlying pacifism is the dream that gathering humanity into a universal society, without fatherlands or different creeds, is the safest means to achieve perpetual peace.[46] "A super co-operative," Plinio Correa de Oliveira notes, "would connect at world level the efforts of peoples; whereas at national level, this would be accomplished by minor cooperatives. This would be an anarchical form of universal republic,"[47] where there would only be "a police force, which will be abolished as soon as scientific and technological advances will have achieved the complete eradication of crime."[48]

Pacifism and tolerantism attach the same value to truth and error—both are subjective expressions of conscience—and are the equivalent of ideological relativism, irenic and destructive ecumenism, and radical skepticism. Everything must be tolerated, except for what opposes the principle of absolute tolerance.

"For men to deserve tolerance, they must begin by not being fanatics," remarks Voltaire,[49] whereas Rousseau states that all opinions and cults may be tolerated, except for Catholic "intolerance," which is guilty of proclaiming the exclusive truth of its Faith. Since, he says, "there can no longer be a single national religion, all those which in turn tolerate the others, must be tolerated. . . . But whoever dare say 'outside the Church there is no salvation' must be expelled from the state."[50]

Hence the ideological, psychological, and bloody persecution of Catholics, waged in the last two centuries by the totalitarianism that was produced by the Enlightenment and the French Revolution. If tolerance is an absolute good, there can be, in fact, one absolute evil only, which is the proclamation of truth. If material peace is the supreme good, the only evil is war, and no war can be permitted other than that against "fundamentalists" who threaten the absolute value of peace. Therefore, the only possible crusade is against those who obstinately proclaim the objective and universal existence of Truth: an implacable "crusade" against the Cross.

Martyrdom: Supreme Assertion of Truth

M artyrdom, "the height of the testimony of moral truth" in the words of Pope John Paul II,[51] is the most radical denial of the relativistic tolerantism. It is also the most perfect act of charity, because it makes us perfect imitators of Jesus according to the Gospel: "For God so loved the world, that he gave his only begotten Son, that whosoever believeth in him should not perish, but have everlasting life" (John 3:16); "Greater love hath no man than this, that a man lay down his life for his friends" (John 15:13).

The concept of martyrdom is intrinsic to Christian life itself. In his great sermon on the mission of the Apostles (Matthew 10), Jesus Christ says: "I send you forth as sheep in the midst of wolves" and predicts, "beware of men: for they will deliver you up to the councils, and they will scourge you in their synagogues; And ye shall be brought before governors and kings for my sake, for a testimony against them and the Gentiles" (verses 16-18).

The specific meaning of the term martyrdom is connected to the concept of "bearing witness," which reaches its climax with the profession of faith christianus sum: "I am Christian."[52] Bearing witness is the essence of martyrdom, and it must be done in public, even up to the point of shedding one's blood. A martyr's witness confirms the witness of the One Who "for this cause came I into the world, that I should bear witness unto the truth" (John 18:37).

What makes a martyr is not a violent death but that his death is inflicted in hatred of Christian truth. It is this that distinguishes the Christian holocaust from any other sacrifice. To be a martyr, someone must be put to death on the grounds of his allegiance to one of the Christian principles of faith or morals, whose infallible master is the Church: In fact, in the words of St. Augustine, "martyres non fecit poena, sed causa"[53] ("It is not death that makes a martyr but the fact that his death and suffering stem from his loyalty to the true faith").

There are truths and moral values, John Paul II teaches, for which one must be prepared to give one's life.[54] Such a witnessing "makes an extraordinarily valuable contribution . . . to warding off a headlong plunge into the most dangerous crisis which can afflict man: the confusion between good and evil, which makes it impossible to build up and to preserve the moral order of individuals and communities. By their eloquent and attractive example of a life completely transfigured by the splendor of moral truth, the martyrs and, in general, all the Church's saints, illuminate every age of history by reawakening its moral sense."[55]

Like any other affliction, martyrdom presupposes fighting. The life of Jesus Christ was an ongoing battle against the coalition of forces hostile to the Kingdom of God: sin, the world, and the devil. Throughout the New Testament, one reads that the life of the Christian is a fight. After all, the original meaning of "Gospel," *eu-anghelion*, is an announcement of a military victory; in this case, Christ's victory over evil and the dark powers.

In his letters, Saint Paul, in particular, uses many metaphors and images drawn from the warrior's life.[56] He explains how the life of the Christian is a *bonum certamen*, a good fight that must be fought "as a good soldier of Jesus Christ" (2 Timothy 2:3). "let us therefore cast off the works of darkness, and let us put on the armour of light" (Romans 13:12). "Put on the whole armour of God, that ye may be able to stand against the wiles of the devil . . . Stand therefore, having your loins girt about with truth, and having on the breastplate of righteousness; And your feet shod with the preparation of the gospel of peace; Above all, taking the shield of faith, wherewith ye shall be able to quench all the fiery darts of the wicked. And take the helmet of salvation, and the sword of the Spirit, which is the word of God" (Ephesians 6:11, 14-17).

The Crusade as a Spiritual Category

Crusade and martyrdom have a common origin; both are profound dimensions of spiritual combat. For the Crusaders, the possibility of martyrdom was evident in their *signum super vestem*, the Cross on their attire which showed that they were prepared to shed their blood fighting against infidels. The combatant for the faith, like the martyr, is he who is prepared to sacrifice his life for Christ, taking to heart the Gospel's words: "For what is a man profited, if he shall gain the whole world, and lose his own soul?" (Matthew 16:26) and "fear not them which kill the body, but are not able to kill the soul: but rather fear him which is able to destroy both soul and body in hell" (Matthew 10:28).

In this respect, the idea of crusade is a permanent category of the Christian soul, which, over time, may fall out of fashion but never disappears. The holy places were again lost; the kingdom of Jerusalem collapsed; the fire of the Crusades seemed to wane; and yet, despite appearances, the idea of crusade did not die. Saints Catherine and Brigid called for a crusade in the 14th century, while Skanderbeg and Hunyadi, in the 15th century, took up arms in the name of a "holy war" against the enemies of Christianity, in the same way as the fighters of Lepanto, Vienna, and Belgrade would do in centuries to follow.[57]

St. Pius V formed a "Holy League" against the Turks that won the historic battle of Lepanto on October 7, 1571. "If medieval insignia, expressing sovereignty, indicate much of the ideal characteristics of medieval sovereignty," Church historian Hubert Jedin writes,

> this applies also to the banners under which the League fought in Lepanto. When Marcantonio Colonna on June 11th, 1571, took his oath in the Papal Chapel, he received from the Pope's hands not only the baton

of commander, but also a red silk flag. Imprinted on the flag was Christ crucified between the princes of Apostles, Peter and Paul; under them were Pius V's coat of arms and the motto "*In hoc signo vinces.*" The crucified Christ is not a mere picture of Christ, but the Cross of the Crusaders itself: Peter and Paul symbolize not only that Colonna is in command of the Papal contingent, but that the Roman Catholic Church and her head, the Pope, identify themselves with the enterprise. The motto "*In hoc signo vinces*" shows how this war was a war for the faith.[58]

A century later, but with a similar spirit, Blessed Innocent XI conducted a holy war against the Turks that led to the liberation of Vienna in 1683 and of Buda in 1686. Pius XI recalls that, beneath Vienna's walls, fighting flared up "not in favor of one single city or of one single empire, but rather for Catholic religion and for Christian civilization in the whole of western Europe."[59] The Blessed Virgin Mary was acknowledged patroness and author of these enterprises. Pius XII reminds us that the Mother of God is the "majestic sovereign of the Church militant," "terrible as *an army* with banners" (Song of Songs 6:10) and is entitled to be honored with the name of "Our Lady of Victories, not unknown in Lepanto and Vienna."[60]

In the 19th century, the spirit of crusade inspired the pontifical Zouaves who rallied in defense of Pius IX. To them, the Pope granted all those indulgences that were given Holy Land Crusaders,[61] and, to the Castelfidardo battle survivors, he donated a medal with the wording "*pro Petri Sede*" ("for the See of Peter") within a silver circle surrounding a Cross of St. Peter, which appears upside down, thus resembling a sword unsheathed for justice. The Pontiff's volunteers did not fight to defend an earthly kingdom but the spiritual supremacy of the Apostolic See, whose freedom and independence was warranted by its status as a sovereign state. In fact, Pius IX always maintained that the offensive against the States of the Church aimed to do away with "the fruit of Redemption and the most holy faith which is the very valuable legacy transmitted to us by the unfathomable sacrifice which took place on the Golgotha."[62]

The Spirit of Crusade in the 21st Century

In the 20th century, perhaps the most atrocious century in the Church's history, a new enemy arose against the Church: communism. Because of its ideological and armed imperialism, it has been aptly described as "the Islam of the 20th century."[63] In his Christmas radio message of 1956, delivered in the wake of the tragic Soviet clampdown in Hungary, Pius XII acknowledged the possibility that a crusade be proclaimed against this enemy in the traditional sense of the word[64]; however, following his death, the Church entered an era of détente and psychological and moral disarmament, up the point of giving back to Islam the standards that were captured in Lepanto and including the Crusades in public requests for pardon.[65]

Yet any condemnation of the Crusades would be tantamount to a condemnation of the papacy itself, which identified itself with them, and a repudiation of a series of pontiffs raised to the altars, such as the blessed Urban II, St. Pius V, and the blessed Innocent XI, who waged and called for "holy wars" to defend Church and Christianity under threat.

Nowadays, at the dawn of the new century, the reign of chaos that is spreading over the planet makes the aspiration to defend Christian civilization all the more important. For this reason, a "Crusader of the 20th century,"[66] Plinio Corrêa de Oliveira, exhorts us to fight "with the courage, perseverance, the determination to tackle and overcome all obstacles, with which the Crusaders marched towards Jerusalem," combating and dying "to restore something which is infinitely worthier than the very valuable shrine of our Savior, namely his sovereignty over souls and Society, which he himself created and saved for them to eternally love him."[67]

John Paul II has proclaimed St. Theresa of the Child Jesus a "doctor of the universal Church,"[68] canonizing her writings and doctrines together with her life. In a moving passage, Saint Theresa, who is talking to Jesus, says she wants to "travel the earth, preach your name and plant your glorious Cross on infidel soil," combining in one single vocation that of the apostle, the crusader, and the martyr. "I feel," she writes, "as if I were called to be a fighter, a priest, an apostle, a doctor, a martyr; as if I could never satisfy the needs of my nature without performing, for your sake, every kind of heroic action at once. I feel as if I'd got the courage to be a Crusader, a Pontifical Zouave, dying on the battlefield in defense of the Church."[69]

"Oh my divine spouse, I'll die in your arms singing, on the battlefield, with the weapon in my hand!"[70] she writes on March 25, 1897; and, a few months later, on August 4, lying on her deathbed, she whispered to her mother superior: "Oh, no, I would not be afraid to go to war. For example, at the time of the Crusades, how happy would I have been to leave and fight against the heretics."[71]

It would be difficult to accuse of being an intolerant fanatic a saint who offered herself in a holocaust to the merciful Love and whom the Church considers "Master in faith and Christian life."[72] Her ardent words help us understand how radically wrong a parallel between the Crusades and *jihad* is, not only as far as the causes and objective goals of the two holy wars are concerned, but also in their respective *animus,* their spirit and conduct; most of all, when one claims to define fundamentalist "fanaticism" as a common denominator of the two.

One can fight out of love or hatred, with an angry heart or with that inner peace that comes when one's faculties are ordered in one's soul; that is when one rests in God, the Lord of peace. St. Bernard of Clairvaux, who dictated the rules of the Templars, wrote, "Tranquil God gives tranquility in all; seeing him peaceful means to be in peace."[73] Inner peace, writes Saint Thomas, in the wake of Saint Augustine, is "the serenity of mind, tranquility of soul, simplicity of heart, the bond of love, the bondage of charity."[74] On the contrary, fanaticism entails a sense of excitement, and therefore derangement, which arises in those who distance themselves from truth and good to follow with all their strength an error, which can be a false religion or the idea, equally false, that all religions are true. In this regard, the spirit of tolerance is far more fanatic than that of crusade, since fanaticism grows in proportion to the hatred of truth and must be defined as a function of it — unless one professes a radical relativism.

Fanaticism is the denial of the spirit of crusade that draws its strength from heroic and peaceful hearts, such as the one of St. Theresa of the Child Jesus.

For over 2,000 years, the Catholic Church has suffered countless attacks and persecutions, but Her worst enemies have always been those who have wanted to extinguish in Her that love of God which prompts a willingness to sacrifice and struggle to defend the supreme assets of faith and Christian civilization.

Endnotes

[1] Peter Partner, *Il Dio degli eserciti. Islam e cristianesimo: le guerre sante* (Turin: Einaudi, 1997; Italian translation), pp. 99–127.

[2] On the sectarian genesis of the concept of tolerance, see, among others, Joseph Lecler, *Storia della tolleranza nel secolo della Riforma* (Brescia: Morcelliana, 1967; Italian translation); Roberto De Mattei, *A sinistra di Lutero. Sette e movimenti religiosi del Cinquecento* (Rome: Città Nuova, 1999).

[3] Franco Cardini, *Studi sulla storia e sull'idea di crociata* (Rome: Jouvence, 1993), p. 169.

[4] Gherard von Rad, *Der heilige Krieg im alten Israel* (Zurich: Zwingli Verlag, 1951), pp. 29 and 49.

[5] Erdmann, *op. cit.*, p. 35; Flori, *op. cit.*, pp. 37-39.

[6] Erdmann, *op. cit.*, p. 35; Villey, *op. cit.*, pp. 21-22.

[7] H.W. Hazard and N.P. Zacour, *The Impact of the Crusades on Europe*, Vol. VI of *A History of the Crusades* (Wisconsin: The University of Wisconsin Press, 1989), p. 33.

[8] Rosalio Castillo Lara, *Coacciòn eclesiastica y Sacro Romano Imperio* (Turin: Pontificio Ateneo Salesiano, 1956), pp. 7-10.

[9] Russell, *op. cit.*, p. 78.

[10] Gratian, *op. cit.*, causa. XXIII, quaestio. 8, p.c. 6, col. 1248

[11] Russell, *op. cit.*, p. 78.

[12] Villey, *op. cit.*, pp. 59-61; Erdmann, *op. cit.*, pp. 181-200; Flori, *op. cit.*, pp. 163-74.

[13] Erdmann, *op. cit.*, p. 186.

[14] Louis Brehier, *"Croisades"* in DAFC (1925), col. 826.

[15] Castillo Lara, *op. cit.*, p. 85.

[16] Saverio Guida, *Canzoni di crociata* (Milan: Oscar Mondatori, 2001), p. 67.

[17] Jean Richard, *L'esprit de la croisade* (Paris: Cerf, 1969), p. 33.

[18] Francois Vallancon, *"De la croisade,"* *Sedes Sapientiae* 53 (Autumn 1995), p. 32.

[19] Guida, *op. cit.*, p. 165.

[20] Paul Alphandery and Alphonse Dupront, *La Cristianità e l'idea di crociata* (Bologna: Il Mulino, 1983; Italian translation), pp. 19–48.

[21] Richard, *op. cit.*, p. 52; Villey, *op. cit.*, pp. 85-88.

[22] Jonathan Riley-Smith, "Crusading as an act of love," *History: The Journal of Historical Association* 65:213 (1980), pp. 177-91.

[23] Pope Eugene III, *Epistola ad Ludovicum regem Galliarum*, 48, in *Epistolae et privilegia* in *PL*, 180, col. 1064.

[24] Richard, *op. cit.*, p. 30.

[25] Castillo Lara, *op. cit.*, pp. 91-92.

[26] *Ibid.*, pp. 92-99.

[27] *Ibid.*, p. 115.

[28] Gianni Baget Bozzo, *Di fronte all'Islam. Il grande conflitto* (Genoa: Marietti, 2001), p. 109.

[29] Nitoglia, *op. cit.*, pp. 24-27.

[30] *Ibid.*, p. 19.

[31] Baget Bozzo, *op. cit.*, p.90.

[32] Noja, *L'Islam.*, p. 146.

[33] Roger Tebib, *L'Ombre de Poitiers. L'intégrisme islamiste dans le monde contemporain*, Volume I of *Traité de la guerre sainte* (Bordeaux: Editions Ulysse, 1988), p. 93; Cantoni, *op. cit.*, pp. 131-32.

[34] Flori, *op. cit.*, p. 348.

[35] *Ibid.*, p. 256.

[36] St. Augustine of Hippo, *Contra litteras Petiliani* (PL,43), book II, 83, 184, col. 315.

[37] St. Thomas Aquinas, *Summa Theologica* II–IIae, quaestio 10, article 8 resp.

[38] Russell, *op. cit.*, p. 199.

[39] Danilo Catarzi, *Teologia delle missioni estere* (Parma: Istituto Saveriano Missioni Estere, 1958), pp. 7-13.

[40] Pope Pius XII, *Discorsi e Radiomessaggi* (June 24, 1944), Vol. VI, pp. 47-52.

[41] See Franco Cardini, *I poveri cavalieri del Cristo. Bernardo di Clairvaux e la fondazione dell'Ordine Templare* (Rimini: Il Cerchio, 1992) for the complete text of *De Laude Novae Militiae*; see also Josè Vincenzo Molle, *I Templari. La regola e gli statuti dell'Ordine* (Genoa: Ecig, 1995) for the Templars' rules and statutes.

[42] Castillo Lara, *op. cit.*, p. 109.

[43] St. Bernard of Clairvaux. *De Laude Novae Militiae* (PL,182), col. 924.

[44] Arthur Veermersch, S.J., *La tolérance* (Paris: Beauchesne, 1912), p. 6; Felix Cappello, S.J., *Summa iuris pubblici ecclesiastici* (Rome: Editio sexta, Gregoriana, 1954), p. 227.

[45] Viktor Cathrein, S.J., *Filosofia morale* (Florence: Libreria Editrice Fiorentina, 1913; Italian translation), p. 381.

[46] Antonio Messineo, "Pacifismo," *Enciclopedia Cattolica*, Vol IX (1952), col. 507.

[47] Plinio Correa de Oliveira, *Trasbordo ideologico inavvertito e dialogo* (Naples: L'Alfiere,1970; Italian translation), p. 73.

[48] Plinio Correa de Oliveira, *Rivoluzione e Contro-Rivoluzione.* (Rome: Luci sull'Est, 1998; Italian translation), p. 82.

[49] Voltaire, *Trattato sulla tolleranza* (Rome: Editori Riuniti, 1995; Italian translation of the 1763 original edition), p. 101.

[50] Jean-Jacques Rousseau, *Du contrat social* (Turin: Einaudi, 1971; Italian translation of the 1762 original edition), pp. 181-82.

[51] Pope John Paul II, *Veritatis Splendor*, n. 93.

[52] Erik Peterson, "Martirio e martire," *Enciclopedia Cattolica*, vol. VIII (1952), col. 235.

[53] St. Augustine of Hippo, *Enarrationes in Psalmos, (PL, 36)*, 13, col. 331.

[54] Pope John Paul II, *Veritatis Splendor*, n. 91–93.

[55] *Ibid.*, n. 93.

[56] Pierre Bourguignon and Francis Wenner, "Combat spiritual," *Dictionnaire de Spiritualité, ascetique et mystique*, Vol. II/1 (1937) cols. 1135-42 ; Bonzi, Umile da Genova, "Combattimento spirituale," *Enciclopedia Cattolica*, Vol. IV (1950), cols. 37-40; Cardini, *Alle radici della cavalleria medioevale*, pp. 178-79; Erdmann, *op. cit.*, pp. 16-17.

[57] Norman Housley, *The Later Crusades, 1274–1580: From Lyons to Alcazar* (Oxford: Oxford University Press, 1992); Jonathan Riley–Smith, *Breve storia delle Crociate* (Milan: Oscar Mondadori, 1994; Italian translation), pp. 275-328; Massimo Viglione, "Il problema della crociata dal II concilio di Lione alla morte di Pio II (1274–1464)," *Ricerche di Storia sociale e religiosa.* XXVII:54 (1998), pp. 201-63.

[58] Hubert Jedin, "Papa Pio V, la Lega Santa e l'idea di crociata" in *Chiesa della fede. Chiesa della storia* (Brescia: Morcelliana, 1972; Italian translation), p. 715.

[59] Pope Pius XI, "Quinquagesimo" letter to Cardinal La Fontaine dated August 30, 1933, in *La pace internazionale* (Rome: Edizioni Paoline, 1962; Italian translation), p. 212.

[60] Pope Pius XII, *Discorsi e Radiomessaggi*, April 21, 1940, Vol. II, p. 86.

[61] Piero Raggi, *La nona crociata. I volontari di Pio IX in difesa di Roma (1860–1870)* (Ravenna: Libreria Tonini, 1992).

[62] Quoted in Roberto de Mattei, *Pio IX* (Casale Monferrato: Piemme, 2000), pp. 97-98.

[63] Jules Monnerot, *Sociologia del comunismo* (Milan: Giuffrè, 1970; Italian translation), pp. 43-187.

[64] Pope Pius XII, *Discorsi e Radiomessaggi*, Christmas radio message to the World on Decem-

ber 23, 1956, Vol. XVIII, pp. 723–42.

[65] See Luigi Accattoli, *Quando il Papa chiede perdono. Tutti i mea culpa di Giovanni Paolo II* (Milan: Mondadori, 1997).

[66] Roberto de Mattei, *The Crusader of the 20th Century: Plinio Correa de Oliveira* (Leominster: Gracewing, 1998).

[67] Plinio Correa de Oliveira, "La crociata del secolo XX" (Italian translation), *Cristianità*, No. 7 (1974), p. 4.

[68] Pope John Paul II, "Apostolic letter for the proclamation of Saint Theresa of the Child Jesus and of the Holy Face as "Doctor of the universal Church," October 19, 1997 (Italian translation) in *Insegnamenti,* Vol. XX, 2 (1997), pp. 616-30.

[69] St. Theresa of Lisieux, *Opere complete* (Vatican City: Libreria Editrice Vaticana, 1997; Italian translation), p. 221.

[70] *Ibid.*, p. 714.

[71] *Ibid.*, pp. 1054–55.

[72] Pope John Paul II, "Apostolic letter for the proclamation of Saint Theresa," *Insegnamenti,* p. 622.

[73] St. Bernard of Clairvaux, *In Cantica (PL, 183),* Sermon 23, 16.

[74] St. Augustine of Hippo, *Sermo 57, De Verbis Domini,* quoted in St. Thomas Aquinas, *In Super Evangelium S. Ioannis lectura* (Turin: Marietti, 1952), p. 368b.

Works Cited

Uda Abd Al-qadir, "La sharia: costituzione fondamentale dei musulmani" in *Dibattito sull'applicazione della sharia* (Turin: Edizioni della Fondazione Giovanni Agnelli, 1995).

Mehdi Abedi and Gary Legenhausen, *Jihad and Shahadat: Struggle and Martyrdom in Islam* (Houston: IRIS, 1986).

Luigi Accattoli, *Quando il Papa chiede perdono. Tutti i mea culpa di Giovanni Paolo II* (Milan: Mondatori, 1997).

Actae Sanctae Sedis (Rome: Typis Poliglottae Officinae).

Al-bukhari, *Detti e Fatti del Profeta dell' Islam* (Turin: Utet, 1982).

Dante Alighieri, *Divina Commedia* (Milan: Rizzoli, 1995; 3 volumes).

Paul Alphandery and Alphonse Dupront, *La Cristianità e l'idea di crociata* (Bologna: Il Mulino, 1983; Italian translation).

Romano Amerio, *Iota unum* (Milan and Naples: Ricciardi, 1985).

H.X. Arquilliere, *Le Augustinisme politique. Essai sur la formation des théories politiques du Moyen Age* (Paris: J. Vrin, 1934).

St. Augustine of Hippo, *De Civitate Dei* (Rome: Città Nuova, 1978-1991; Latin with Italian translation, 3 volumes).

—, *Contra Faustum Manichaeum* (PL, 42).

—, *Contra litteras Petiliani* (PL,43).

—, *Enarrationes in Psalmos* (PL, 36).

—, *Epistola ad Marcellinum* (PL, 33).

—, *Epistola al conte Bonifacio* (PL, 33).

—, *Quaestiones in Heptateuchum* (PL, 34).

Gianni Baget Bozzo, *Di fronte all'Islam. Il grande conflitto* (Genoa: Marietti, 2001).

St. Bernard of Clairveaux, *In Cantica* (PL, 183).

—, *De Laude Novae Militiae* (PL, 182).

Giovanni Bonzi (a.k.a. Umile Da Genova), "Combattimento spirituale," *Enciclopedia Cattolica* (Vol. IV, 1950).

Pierre Bourguignon and Francis Wenner, "Combat spiritual," *Dictionnaire de Spiritualité, ascetique et mystique* (Vol. II/1, 1937).

Paolo Branca, *Voci dell'Islam moderno. Il pensiero arabo-mussulmano fra rinnovamento e tradizione* (Genoa: Marietti, 1997).

—, *Introduzione all'Islam* (Cinisello Balsamo: San Paolo, 1995).

Louis Brehier, "Croisades" (*DAFC*, 1925).

Yves de la Briere, S.J., "Paix et Guerre" (*DAFC*, Vol. III, 1926).

—, *Le droit de juste guerre, Tradition thèologique, adaptations contemporaines* (Paris: A. Pedone, 1938).

Claude Cahen, "Dimma," *Encyclopédie de l'Islam* (Vol. II, 1965).

Rino Cammilleri, *I santi militari* (Casale Monferrato: Piemme, 1992).

Giovanni Cantoni, *Aspetti in ombra della legge sociale dell'Islam. Per una critica della vulgata "islamicamente corretta"* (S. Cataldo, Caltanissetta: Centro Studi sulla Cooperazione "A. Cammarata," 2000).

Felix Cappello, S.J., *Summa iuris pubblici ecclesiastici* (Rome: Editio sexta, Gregoriana, 1954).

Franco Cardini, *Alle radici della cavalleria medioevale* (Florence: La Nuova Italia, 1982).

— , *I poveri cavalieri del Cristo. Bernardo di Clairvaux e la fondazione dell'Ordine Templare* (Rimini: Il Cerchio, 1992).

— , *Studi sulla storia e sull'idea di crociata* (Rome: Jouvence, 1993).

Olivier Carré, *L'Islam et l'Etat dans le monde aujourd'hui* (Paris: PUF, 1982).

Rosalio Castillo Lara, *Coacciòn eclesiastica y Sacro Romano Imperio* (Turin: Pontificio Ateneo Salesiano, 1956).

Danilo Catarzi, *Teologia delle missioni estere* (Parma: Istituto Saveriano Missioni Estere, 1958).

Catechismo Maggiore promulgato da S. Pio X (Milan: Ares, 1979).

Catechismo della Chiesa Cattolica (Vatican City: Libreria Editrice Vaticana, 1992).

Viktor Cathrein, S.J., *Filosofia morale* (Florence: Libreria Editrice Fiorentina, 1913; Italian translation).

Chafik Cherata, "Dhimma" in Vol. II of *Encyclopédie de l'Islam* (Paris: new edition, E.J. Brill and G.P. Maisonneuve & Larosa, Leyde, 1960-1998).

Plinio Correa de Oliveira, *Trasbordo ideologico inavvertito e dialogo* (Naples: L'Alfiere, 1970; Italian translation).

— , "La crociata del secolo XX" (Italian translation), *Cristianità* (No. 7, 1974).

— , *Rivoluzione e Contro-Rivoluzione* (Rome: Luci sull'Est, 1998; Italian Translation).

DACL = *Dictionnaire d'Archéologie Chrétienne et de Liturgie* (Paris : Letouzey et Ané, 1907-1953; 30 volumes).

DAFC = *Dictionnaire Apologétique de la Foi Catholique* (Paris: Beauchesne, 1925-1931; 4 volumes).

Felice Dassetto and Alberto Bastenier, *Europa: Nuova frontiera dell'Islam* (Rome: Edizioni del Lavoro, 1991).

DDC = *Dictionnaire de Droit Canonique* (Paris: Letouzey et Ané, 1935-1958; 7 volumes).

Etienne Delaruelle, "Essai sur la formation de l'idée de croisade," *Bullettin de littérature ecclésiastique*, XLII (1941): 24-45, 86-103; XLV (1944): 13-46, 73-90; LIV (1953): 226-239; LV (1954); 50-63, now in *L'idée de croisade au Moyen Age* (Turin: Bottega d'Erasmo, 1980).

— , "L'idée de croisade in Saint Bernard," *Melanges Saint Bernard*, Dijon 1953, now in *L'idée de croisade au Moyen Age* (Turin: Bottega d'Erasmo, 1980).

Massimo de Leonardis, *Europa–Stati Uniti: un Atlantico più largo?* (Milan: Franco Angeli, 2001).

Alexandre Del Valle, *L'Islamisme et les Etats–Unis. Une alliance contre l'Europe* (Lausanne: L'Age d'Homme, 1997).

— , *Guerres contre l'Europe. Bosnie-Kosovo-Tchétchénie . . .* (Paris: Editions des Syrtes, 2000).

Roberto de Mattei, *Il crociato del secolo XX. Plinio Correa de Oliveira* (Casale Monferrato: Piemme, 1996).

— , *A sinistra di Lutero. Sette e movimenti religiosi del Cinquecento* (Rome: Città Nuova, 1999).

— , *Pio IX* (Casale Monferrato: Piemme, 2000).

— , *La sovranità necessaria. Riflessioni sulla crisi dello Stato moderno* (Rome: Il Minotauro, 2001).

Antonio D'emilia, "Editto di Medina," *Novissimo Digesto Italiano* (Turin: UTET, 1964; vol VI).

— , *Scritti di diritto islamico* (Rome: Istituto per l'Oriente, 1976; collated by Francesco Castro).

Alois Dempf, *Sacrum Imperium* (Florence: Le Lettere, 1988; Italian translation).

Dibattito sull'applicazione della Shari'a (Turin: Edizioni della Fondazione Giovanni Agnelli, 1995).

DSp = *Dictionnaire de Spiritualité catholique* (Paris: Beauchesne, 1937-1994; 16 volumes).

DTC = *Dictionnaire de Théologie Catholique* (Paris: Letouzey et Ané, 1909-1972; 33 volumes).

Enciclopedia Cattolica (Florence: Sansoni, 1949-1954; 12 volumes).

Encyclopédie de l'Islam (Paris: new edition, E. J.Brill and G.P.Maisonneuve & Larose, Leyde, 1960-1998; 10 volumes).

Carl Erdmann, *Alle origini dell'idea di crociata* (Spoleto: Centro italiano di studi sull'Alto Medioevo, 1996).

Bruno Etienne, *L'Islamismo radicale* (Milan: Rizzoli, 1988).

Pope Eugene III, *Epistola ad Ludovicum regem Galliarum*, 48, in *Epistolae et privilegia* in *PL*, 180.

Antoine Fattal, *Le Statut Lègal de non-musulmans en pays d'Islam* (Beirut: Imprimerie catholique, 1958).

Guillaume Faye, *La colonisation de l'Europe. Discours vrai sur l'immigration et l'Islam* (Paris: L'Encre, 2000).

Silvio Ferrari, *L'Islam in Europa. Lo statuto giuridico della comunità mussulmana* (Bologna: Il Mulino, 1996).

Valeria Fiorani Piacentini, "Il pensiero militare nel mondo islamico," vol. I, "Credenti e non credenti: il pensiero militare e la dottrina del jihad," *Rivista Militare* (1991).

Jean Flori, *La guerre sainte. La formation de l'idée de la Croisade dans l'Occident chrétien* (Paris: Aubier, 2001).

Robert Folz, *Etude sur le culte liturgique de Charlemagne dans les églises de l'Empire* (Geneva: Slatkine rpt, 1973).

Ramon Garcia de Haro, *La vita cristiana. Corso di teologia morale fondamentale* (Milan: Ares, 1995).

Louis Gardet, *La Cité Musulmane. Vie sociale et politique* (Paris: Vrin, 1981; enhanced edition).

Pope Gelasius I, *Epistula VIII ad Anastasium Imperatorem* (PL, 59).

François Gere, *La guerre psychologique* (Paris: Economica, 1997).

Carlo Giacon, S.J., *La seconda scolastica. I problemi giuridico–politici. Suarez, Bellarmino, Mariana* (Milan: Fratelli Bocca, 1950; 3 volumes).

Jean-Luc Giorda, "Ma esiste un Islam moderato?" *Il Tempo* (October 11, 2001).

Ignaz Goldziher, *Le dogme et la loi de l'Islam* (Paris: P. Geuthner, 1920).

— , *Muslim Studies* (London: George Allen & Unwin, 1967; 2 volumes).

Gratian, *Decretum, emendatum et variis lectionibus simul et notationibus illustratum* (PL, 187).

Saverio Guida, *Canzoni di crociata* (Milan: Oscar Mondatori, 2001).

Renzo Guolo, *Il partito di Dio. L'Islam radicale contro l'Occidente* (Milan: Guerini e Associati, 1994).

— , *Avanguardia della fede. L'Islamismo tra ideologia e politica* (Milan: Guerini e Associati, 1999).

H.W. Hazard and N.P. Zacour, *A History of the Crusades*, Vol. VI, *The Impact of the Crusades on Europe*. (Wisconsin: The University of Wisconsin Press, 1989).

Jacques Heers, *Les Barbaresques. La corse et la guerre en Méditerranée, XIV-XVI siécles* (Paris: Perrin, 2001).

Charles Joseph Hefele, *Histoire des Conciles d'aprés les documents originaux* (Paris: Letouzey et Anè, 1907).

Norman Housley, *The Later Crusades, 1274-1580. From Lyons to Alcazar* (Oxford: Oxford University Press, 1992).

Samuel P. Huntington, *The Clash of Civilizations and the Remaking of World Order* (New York: Simon and Schuster, 2003).

Insegnamenti pontifici. La pace internazionale, Parte prima: *La guerra moderna*. (Rome: Edizioni Paoline, 1962; Italian translation).

Hubert Jedin, "Papa Pio V, la Lega Santa e l'idea di crociata" in *Chiesa della fede. Chiesa della storia* (Brescia: Morcelliana, 1972; Italian translation).

John Paul II, "Messaggio per la Giornata Mondiale della Pace–1 January 1981" in *Messaggi di pace: I discorsi integrali per la Giornata Mondiale della Pace dal 1968 al 1999* (Cantalupa and Turin: Effatà editrice, 1999).

— , "Messaggio per la Giornata Mondiale della Pace–1 January 1982" in *Messaggi di pace: I discorsi integrali per la Giornata Mondiale della Pace dal 1968 al 1999* (Cantalupa and Turin: Effatà editrice, 1999).

— , *Veritatis Splendor*, Italian translation in *Insegnamenti* (Vatican City: Libreria Editrice Vaticana, 1995).

— , "Apostolic letter for the proclamation of Saint Theresa of the Child Jesus and of the Holy Face as 'Doctor of the universal Church,'" Italian translation in *Insegnamenti* (Vol. XX, 2, 1997).

— , "Message dated 14 December 2000," *Osservatore Romano*, 51 (December 22, 2000).

Ernst Kantorowicz, *The king's Two Bodies: A study in Mediaeval Political Theology* (Princeton: Princeton University Press, 1957).

Joseph Lecler, *Storia della tolleranza nel secolo della Riforma.* (Brescia: Morcelliana, 1967; 2 volumes, Italian translation).

Henri Leclercq, "Militarisme," *DACL*, volume XI (1933).

Bernard Lewis, *The Muslim Discovery of Europe* (New York: Norton and Company, 1991).

— , *La rinascita islamica* (Bologna: Il Mulino, 1991; Italian translation).

— , *The Political Language of Islam* (Chicago: The University of Chicago Press, 1991).

— , *Islam and the West* (New York: Oxford University Press, 1993).

— , *The Crisis of Islam: Holy War and Unholy Terror* (New York: Random House, 2003).

William S. Lind, "Defending Western Culture," *Foreign Policy* 84: (Fall 1991).

S.A.A. Mawdudi, *The Islamic Law and Constitution* (Lahore: Islamic Publications Ltd, 1975).

Ali Merad, *L'Islam Contemporain* (Paris: Presses Univesitaries de France, 1995).

Messaggi di pace: I discorsi integrali per la Giornata Mondiale della Pace dal 1968 al 1999 (Cantalupa and Turin: Effatà editrice, 1999).

Antonio Messineo, "Guerra," *Enciclopedia Cattolica*, Volume VI (1952).

— , "Pacifismo," *Enciclopedia Cattolica*, Volume IX (1952).

Johannes Messner, *Etica social,politica y economica a la luz del derecho natural* (Madrid: Rialp, 1967).

Richard P. Mitchell, *The Society of Muslim Brothers*. (Oxford: Oxford University Press, 1969).

Josè Vincenzo Molle, *I Templari. La regola e gli statuti dell'Ordine* (Genoa: Ecig, 1995).

Jules Monnerot, *Sociologia del comunismo* (Milan: Giuffrè, 1970; Italian translation of original edition of 1949).

Anna Maria Morisi, *La guerra nel pensiero cristiano dalle origini alle crociate.* (Florence: Sansoni, 1963).

Sachiko Murata and William C. Chittick, *The Vision of Islam* (St.Paul, MN: Paragon House, 1994).

Hala Mustafa, "L'Islam politico in Egitto: il richiamo sull'applicazione della sharia'ah dei movimenti islamici radicali.," *Dibattito sull'applicazione della Shari'a, op. cit.*

Carlo Alfonso Nallino, *Raccolta di scritti editi e inediti*, Vol. III, *Storia dell'Arabia preislamica. Storia e instituzioni musulmane* (Rome: Istituto per l'Oriente, 1941).

Stefano Nitoglia, *Islam, Anatomia di una setta* (Milan: Effedieffe, 1994).

Sergio Noja, *Maometto* (Fossano: Editrice Esperienze, 1974).

— , *L'Islam e il suo Corano* (Milan: Mondadori, 1988).

— , *Maometto profeta dell'Islam* (Milan: Mondadori, 1991).

Novissimo Digesto italiano (Turin: UTET, 1960; Vol. VI).

T. Ortolan, "Guerre," *DTC* (1925; Vol. VI, 2).

Alfredo Ottaviani, *Institutiones iuris publici ecclesastici* (Vatican City: Typis Polyglottis Vaticanis, 1958 — IV edition, *emendata et aucta*; 2 volumes).

J. Vatikiotis Panayotis, *Islam: stati senza nazioni* (Milan: Il Saggiatore, 1993; Italian translation).

Rinaldo Panetta, *I saraceni in Italia* (Milan: Mursia, 1998).

Jean de Pange, *Le Roi très-chrétien* (Paris: Arma Artis, 1985).

Peter Partner, *Il Dio degli eserciti. Islam e cristianesimo: le guerre sante* (Turin: Einaudi, 1997; Italian translation).

Luciano Perena Vicente, *Teoria de la Guerra en Francisco Suarez* (Madrid: C.S.I.C., 1954).

Rudolph Peters, *Jihad in Classical and Modern Islam* (Princeton: Markus Wiener, 1996).

Erik Peterson, "Martirio e martire," *Enciclopedia Cattolica,* Vol. VIII (1952).

Pius XI, "Quinquagesimo" letter to Cardinal La Fontane, August 30, 1933, in *La pace internazionale.*

Pius XII, *Discorsi e Radiomessaggi* (Vatican City: Tipografia Vaticana, 1959; 21 volumes).

— , Encyclical *"Summi Pontificatus,"* October 20, 1939, *op. cit.,* Volume III.

— , Speech dated April 21, 1940, *op. cit.,* Vol. II.

— , Speech dated June 24, 1944, *op. cit.,* Vol. VI.

— , Radio message to the world dated December 24, 1948, Vol. X.

Pius XII, Encyclical *"Summi Maeroris,"* July 19, 1950, *op. cit.,* Vol. XIII.

— , Speech dated October 19, 1953, *op. cit.,* Vol. XV.

— , Speech dated September 30, 1954, *op. cit.,* Vol. XVI.

— , Christmas radio message to the world, December 23, 1956, *op. cit.,* Vol. XVIII.

PL = *Patrologiae Cursus Completus, Series Latina,* edited by Jean-Paul Migne (Paris: Firmin-Didot, 1857-1926; 161 volumes).

Gherard von Rad, *Der heilige Krieg im alten Israel* (Zurich: Zwingli Verlag, 1951).

Piero Raggi, *La nona crociata. I volontari di Pio IX in difesa di Roma (1860-1870)* (Ravenna: Libreria Tonini, 1992).

Jean Richard, *L'esprit de la croisade* (Paris: Cerf, 1969).

Jonathan Riley-Smith, "Crusading as an act of love," *History: The Journal of Historical Association*, 65: 213 (1980).

– , *Breve storia delle Crociate* (Milan: Oscar Mondadori, 1994; Italian translation.)

Jean-Jacques Rousseau, *Du contrat social* (Turin: Einaudi, 1971; Italian translation of the 1762 original).

Olivier Roy, *Généalogie de l'Islamisme* (Paris: Hachette, 1995).

Frederick H. Russell, *The Just War in the Middle Ages* (London and New York: Cambridge University Press,1975).

Halim Sabit Sibay, "Jihad," in *Encyclopédie de l'Islam*, Vol. II (1965).

M. Josef Stamer, *L'Islam en Afrique au sud du Sahara* (Koeningstein: Aide à l'Eglise en Détresse, 1995).

Francisco Suarez, *Opera Omnia* (Paris: Vivés, 1856-1878; 26 Volumes).

Roger Tebib, *Traité de la guerre sainte*, Vol. I, *L'Ombre de Poitiers. L'intégrisme islamiste dans le monde contemporain* (Bordeaux: Editions Ulysse, 1988).

St. Theresa of Lisieux, *Opere complete* (Vatican City: Libreria Editrice Vaticana, 1997).

St. Thomas Aquinas, *Summa Theologica* (Bologna: Edizioni Studio Domenicano, 1984; Latin with Italian translation, 35 volumes).

– , *In Super Evangelium S. Ioannis lectura* (Turin: Marietti, 1952).

James Turner Johnson, *The Holy War Idea in Western and Islamic Tradition* (University Park, PA: the Pennsylvania State University Press, 1997).

François Vallancon, "De la croisade," *Sedes Sapientiae*, 53 (Autumn 1995).

Martin Van Creveld, *The Transformation of War* (New York: The Free Press, 1991).

Alfred Vanderpol, *La doctrine scolastique du droit de guerre* (Paris: A. Pedone, 1919) .

Achille Varzi, "Asimmetria il disordine mondiale," *La Stampa*.(November 2, 2001).

Vatican Ecumenical Council II, *Pastoral Constitution on the Church in the Modern World "Gaudium at Spes"* (Vatican, December 7, 1965).

Arthur Veermersch, S.J., *La tolérance* (Paris: Beauchesne, 1912).

Giorgio Vercellin, *L'Islam e la guerra* (Florence: Giunti, 1997).

Massimo Viglione, "Il problema della crociata dal II concilio di Lione alla morte di Pio II (1274-1464) con relativa bibliografia," *Ricerche di Storia sociale e religiosa*, XXVII: 54 (1998).

Michael Villey, *La Croisade. Essai sur la formation d'une theorie juridique* (Paris: Vrin, 1942).

Voltaire, *Trattato sulla tolleranza* (Rome: Editori Riuniti, 1995; Italian translation of the 1763 original).

Montgomery Watt, *Islamic Political Thought* (Edinburgh: Edinburgh University Press, 1980).

— , *Breve storia dell'Islam* (Bologna: Il Mulino, 2001).

Eberhard Welty, *Catechismo Sociale* (Francavilla, Chieti: Paoline, 1966; 2 volumes, Italian translation).

Bat Ye'or, *Juifs et Chrétiens sous l'Islam. Les dhimmis face au défi intègriste* (Paris: Berg International, 1994).

ABOUT THE AUTHORS

Roberto de Mattei

Roberto de Mattei is a professor of modern history at the University of Cassino; professor of the history of Christianity at the European University of Rome; vice president of the National Research Council; special advisor to the Italian government for foreign affairs; president of Centro Culturale Lepanto (Lepanto Cultural Center), Rome; editor of the international review *Nova Historica*; member of the international advisory board of the European Foundation, London; and member of the Board of Guarantors of the Italian Academy for Advanced Studies in America at Columbia University.

He is the author of 16 books, translated into various languages, including *A sinistra di Lutero* (*To the left of Luther*); *The Crusader of the XX Century: Plinio Corrêa de Oliveira*; *Pius IX*; and *La souveraineté nécessaire*.

Karl Keating

A former lawyer, Karl Keating is the founder and president of Catholic Answers, one of the largest lay-run apostolates of Catholic apologetics and evangelization in the United States, and the founding editor of *This Rock*. He has been a columnist for the *National Catholic Register* and the *Canadian Catholic Review* and has written for many other publications. He is the author of several books, including *Catholicism and Fundamentalism*; *Controversies: High Level Catholic Apologetics*; *What Catholics Really Believe*; *Nothing But the Truth*; and *The Usual Suspects*.

Printed in the United States
201187BV00004B/13-60/A

9 780972 061650